SACRED AND HOUSEHOLD

POETRY,

GATHERED FROM THE

HIGHWAYS AND BY-WAYS.

BY THE COMPILER OF "LIFE AND LETTERS OF MISS MARY C. GREENLEAF."

"Oh, lay it lowly at His blessed feet;
Have thou the honor thus thy Lord to greet,
And join thy voice unto the angel choir,
From out his secret altar touched with hallowed fire."
[MILTON.

NEWBURYPORT:
PUBLISHED FOR THE COMPILER BY MOULTON & CLARK.
BOSTON: BROWN, TAGGARD & CHASE.
1858.

INVOCATION.

UNTO Thy shrine, my GOD, my King,
This votive offering I bring;
This song where many voices blend!
To Thee, to Thee may it ascend!

Its every fault do Thou atone,
Dear SAVIOUR, bear it to the throne—
And may the unequal notes we raise
Wake sweeter echoes to Thy praise!

And Thou, our COMFORTER and Guide!
Oh, ever in our souls abide—
Our songs with purer love inspire,
Until we join the seraphic choir.

CONTENTS.

INDEX OF FIRST LINES.

INTRODUCTION.

STEARNE has somewhere remarked, with a degree of justice, that the process of book-making in modern times, was little more than pouring from one bottle into another. In truth, so little *thinking* have the ancients left us to do, that a student of the last century, at Dartmouth, used despairingly to exclaim, "If I could only *originate* one single idea, I should die happy!" If there is really such a paucity of new ideas, in this age of new inventions, as these gentlemen seem to imply, then the mere compiler need not feel that his office, humble though it may be deemed, falls so far below that of the author. He only does that avowedly, which the latter does perhaps unconsciously.

The compiler of a volume of sacred poetry has in these days a delightful task. To collect and preserve in one little casket those scattered gems which lie hid in the sands of our literature, some of which a few more tides might wash away but for his or her quick eye, and gathering hand, and to give them to the light, is surely no ungrateful office. But the gems of *sacred* poetry are comparatively rare. Love, and beauty, and the fading things of earth are worshipped in the sweetest strains — but the highest love and the most glorious beauty are, by most of those called the standard poets, neglected. Yet is this neglect a violence to man's best nature. Truth and beauty are always in harmony. Divine truth and poetic beauty are in the fullest harmony. Poetic beauty pervades the inspired Word. From the sublime glory of the opening page of Sacred History, when God said, "Let there be light, and light was," to the closing picture of the New Jerusalem shining upon us in unearthly radiance, the whole Scripture, while it is eternal truth of such solemn interest to us, is also a dramatic poem of transcendant grandeur and beauty. Poetic beauty pervades the visible universe. It literally "glows in the stars and blossoms in the trees." And the soul of man responds to it. It calls him to adoring songs in honor of its Divine Author; and even the natural heart feels after Him, and reaches upward, and would fain dissever Divine Truth from Divine Beauty, and adore the one while it bows not to the other. Moore and Willis are sad, sad examples of this. But the Christian responds with his whole soul to the call. To him, "Day unto day uttereth speech, and night unto night showeth knowledge." "No speech, no language, voice is not heard;" yet does he apprehend those *words* which *are gone out to the end of the world*, and they are to him both music and poetry; — and all the poetic numbers of the songs of Zion are but the faint echoes of that high melody which breathes through all the works of the perfect ONE.

This little collection consists chiefly of the cuttings and transcribings of former years. Resolving that my treasures should no longer remain a monopoly, I have made further selections, and have the pleasure of inserting a number of beautiful pieces never before published. Would that I were permitted to give the names of the lovely ladies to whom four of them are due.

Several others will, it is believed, be new to the American reader. They were found among a large number of English sheet tracts in verse, which have been recently selected by a lady residing in London, and sent to her relatives in this city.

Slight attempt has been made at systematic arrangement. It is deemed, that the course of poetic sentiment and feeling should not, like that of the canal, be confined and guided to suit a specific, practical purpose. Rather, like the river, let it wind along, at its own sweet will, through green meadows and fertile valleys — through the dark and tangled wilderness, and dashing over rocks and precipices, let it ripple and murmur about the very towers and battlements of the King of Terrors; — so it may but reflect the warm beams of the SUN of Righteousness — so the Star of Peace and Hope — the Star of Bethlehem, shines up through its clear depths, it is enough. If in rare instances, it reflect only the light, but not the direct rays of that SUN, let it be forgiven.

As I write, sits beside me, one whose "crown of glory" is not yet exchanged for the one he will cast at the feet of his Saviour. I am not indifferent to the good opinion of the public; but if this little work meet his approval, my more earnest wish will be fulfilled.

That it may do good — that it may cheer the heart and bless the soul, thus glorifying our Father in Heaven, should be the chief and ultimate aim of this and every similar attempt. But, alas, how few of us have the single eye! Yet who can tell that some word here found may not arrest the eye, and touch the heart of one now far from truth and happiness — that the song may not win the soul guarded against the sermon! Who can tell that by something herein contained, the wanderer *in* as well as from the path of Life, may not be recalled! Reader, let us unite in the earnest aspiration that this may be one among the countless instrumentalities in the hand of our loving and wise Master by which he draws us to himself.

E. DANA.

NEWBURYPORT, Nov. 1858.

Sacred and Household Poetry.

FOUNTAIN OF SILOAM.

REV. R. M. M'CHEYNE.

BENEATH Moriah's rocky side
A gentle fountain springs;
Silent and soft its waters glide,
Like the peace the Spirit brings.

The thirsty Arab stoops to drink
Of the cool and quiet wave,
And the thirsty spirit stops to think
Of Him who came to save.

Siloam is the fountain's name,
It means "one sent from God;"
And thus the holy Saviour's fame
It gently spreads abroad.

2

O grant that I, like this sweet well,
May Jesus' image bear,
And spend my life, my all, to tell
How full his mercies are!

Foot of Carmel, June, 1839.

HYMN TO THE SAVIOUR.

Thou, who didst stoop below
To drain the cup of woe,
Wearing the form of frail mortality;
Thy blessed labors done,
Thy crown of victory won,
Hast passed from earth---passed to thy throne on high.

Man may no longer trace
In thy celestial face
The image of the bright, the viewless one;
Nor may thy servants hear,
Save with faith's raptured ear,
Thy voice of tenderness, — God's holy Son!

Our eyes behold thee not,
Yet hast thou not forgot

Those who have placed their hope, their trust in
thee;
Before thy Father's face
Thou hast prepared a place,
That where thou art, there may they also be.

It was no path of flowers,
Through this dark world of ours,
Beloved of the Father, thou didst tread;
And shall we in dismay
Shrink from the narrow way,
When clouds and darkness are around it spread?

O Thou who art our life,
Be with us through the strife;
Was not thy head by earth's fierce tempests
bowed?
Raise then our eyes above,
To see a Father's love
Beam, like a bow of promise, through the cloud.

E'en through the awful gloom,
Which hovers o'er the tomb,
That light of love our guiding star shall be;
Our spirits shall not dread
The shadowy way to tread,
Friend! Guardian! Saviour! which doth lead to
Thee!

PRAISE TO GOD.

Thou who createdst all! Thou fountain
  Of our sun's light — who dwellest far
  From man beyond the farthest star,
Yet ever present; who dost heed
Our spirits in their utmost need;
  We bless thee, Father, that we *are!*

We bless thee for our inward life;
  For its immortal date decreeing;
For that which comprehendeth thee,
A spark of thy divinity,
  Which is the being of our being!

We bless thee for this bounteous earth;
  For its increase; for corn and wine,
For forest oaks, for mountain rills,
For cattle on a thousand hills,
  We bless thee, for all good is thine!

The earth is thine, and it thou keepest,
  That man may labor not in vain;
Thou giv'st the grass, the grain, the tree,
Seed time and harvest come from thee,
  The early and the latter rain!

The earth is thine — the summer earth,
  Fresh with the dews, with sunshine bright;

With golden clouds in evening hours,
With singing birds, and balmy flowers,
  Creatures of beauty and delight.

The earth is thine — thy creature, man!
  Thine are all worlds, all suns that shine;
Darkness and light, and life and death,
Whate'er all space inhabiteth —
  Creator! Father! all is thine!

THE THORN.

Our Saviour wore a crown of thorn
  With not one rose entwined;
And more did this sad crown adorn
  Than that he left behind;
And gladly did he press it there
  Upon his God-like brow,
Knowing that in our path more fair
  Would bloom the roses now.

O, when we grasp the fragrant flowers
  That throw such beauty round,
And murmur 'midst our blushing bowers,
  That still a thorn is found,—

O let us think of Him who wore
 The thorn without the rose,
And bear, as patiently He bore,
 Our *fewer*, *lighter* woes.

NOT ON A PRAYERLESS BED.

Not on a prayerless bed, not on a prayerless bed,
 Compose thy weary limbs to rest;
 For they alone are blest
  With balmy sleep
  Whom angels keep.
 Not, though by care oppressed,
  Or thought of anxious sorrow,
 Or thought, in many a coil perplexed
  For coming morrow —
  Lay not thy head
  On prayerless bed!

For who can say, when sleep thine eyes shall close,
 That earthly cares and woes
 To thee may e'er return?
  Rouse up, my soul,
  Slumber control,
 And let thy lamp burn brightly;

So shall thine eyes discern
Things pure and rightly;
Taught by the spirit's beam,
Never on prayerless bed
To lay thine unblest head.

Bethink thee, slumbering soul, of all that's promised
To faith and holy prayer!
Lives there within thy breast
A worm that gives unrest?
Ask peace from Heaven; —
Peace will be given:
Humble self-love and pride
Before the Crucified,
Who for thy sins has died;
Nor lay thy weary head
Upon a prayerless bed!

Hast thou no pining want, nor wish, nor care,
That calls for holy prayer?
Has thy day been so bright,
That, in its flight,
There is no trace of sorrow?
And, art thou sure to-morrow
Will be like to-day, and more
Abundant? Dost thou lay up store,
And still make place for more?

Thou fool! this very night
Thy soul may wing its flight.

Hast thou no being than thyself more dear,
Who tracks the ocean deep,
And when storms sweep
The wintry skies,
For whom thou wak'st and weepest?
Oh! when thy pangs are deepest,
Seek then the covenant ark of Prayer,
For He that slumbereth not is *there!*
His ears are open to thy cries!
Oh! then on prayerless bed
Lay not thy thoughtless head!

Hast thou no loved one than thyself more dear,
Who claims a prayer from thee?
Some who ne'er bend the knee
From infidelity?
Think, if by prayer they 're brought—
Thy prayer, to be forgiven,
And making peace with Heaven,
Unto the cross they 're led!
Oh, for their sakes, on prayerless bed
Lay not thy unblest head!

Arouse thee, weary soul, nor yield to slumber,
Till in communion blest,

With the elect thou rest —
Those souls of countless number;
And with them, raise
The note of praise,
Reaching from earth to heaven,
Chosen, redeemed, forgiven:
So lay thy happy head,
Prayer-crowned, on blessed bed!

THE WATER OF LIFE.

Peace for the troubled soul!
Balm for the wounded heart!
Here the pure waters roll
Which healing power impart;
Here blooms the fruit of Life's immortal tree;
Come, child of sorrow! for it blooms for thee!

Earth's troubled streams forsake, —
Her sin-polluted rills;
Thy thirst they cannot slake:
From yonder heavenly hills
Flows the bright river of eternal joy,
The only bliss unmingled with alloy.

Then come without a fear,
The stream of Life is free;
Let hope thy spirit cheer,
Its waters flow for thee!
Here wash away thy sorrow and thy sin;
So shall thy peace, thy blessedness begin.

I DIE DAILY.

When on my pillow'd couch I lay
Each night this weary head of mine,
And think upon the by-gone day, —
Its tangled thread of thought untwine,
I seem another life to leave,
And born at morn, to die at eve.

Each day, O Father, is a life,—
Each, the great whole's epitome,
With passion stirr'd, with action rife,
Prank'd with capricious pain and glee.
Hours fly for years, nor growing age
Lacks here its monitory stage.

Morn, from thy hand's renewing power,
Brings me, as from the womb again,

Fresh as the babe in natal hour,
   Unsoiled as yet with worldly stain.
My heart is calm, my breast is clear,
And lively to thy voice, my ear.

Then Noon, like manhood, bears along,
   Ah! far from innocence and home,
To push, amid the worldly throng,
   'Mid scenes of bustling guilt to roam;
And toil, and care, and guile and sin,
O'erpower thy voice, with deafening din.

Then Eve, meet type of mellowing age,
   'Mid dying sounds, and growing calm,
Calls me to home, and musing sage:
   Cool as her dews, thy SPIRIT's balm
Pours on my fevered heart, and full
Thy voice, on ears no longer dull.

Then Night, like death, as in the grave,
   Lays down my aching head once more,
Blessing the bounteous hand which gave,
   Praying the taker to restore;
I close upon the world my sight,
And sink amid surrounding night.

Great Giver of this mortal breath,
   Which thou hast roused again to sing,

O, through a daily life and death,
  Conduct me still, Almighty King!
Death to some sin, my shame of yore, —
Life to some grace, unfelt before.

EVENING HYMN.

Father! by thy love and power
Comes again the evening hour:
Light has vanished, labors cease,
Weary creatures rest in peace.
Thou, whose genial dews distil
  On the lowliest weed that grows,
Father! guard our couch from ill,
  Lull thy children to repose.
We to thee ourselves resign,
Let our latest thoughts be thine.

Saviour! to thy Father bear
This our feeble evening prayer;
Thou hast seen how oft to-day
We, like sheep, have gone astray;
Worldly thoughts, and thoughts of pride,
  Wishes to thy cross untrue,
Secret faults, and undescried,

  Meet thy spirit-piercing view,
Blessed Saviour! yet through thee
Pray that these may pardoned be.

Holy Spirit! breath of balm!
Fall on us in evening's calm:
Yet awhile before we sleep,
We, with thee, will vigils keep;
Lead us on our sins to muse,
  Give us truest penitence,
Then the love of God infuse,
  Breathing humble confidence;
Melt our spirits, mould our will,
Soften, strengthen, comfort still!

Blessed Trinity! be near
Through the hours of darkness drear:
When the help of man is far,
Ye more clearly present are:
Father, Son, and Holy Ghost,
  Watch o'er our defenceless head;
Let your Angels' guardian host
  Keep all evil from our bed,
Till the flood of morning rays
Wake us to a song of praise.

THE CHILD AND THE MOURNERS.

CHARLES MACKAY, LL. D.

A little child beneath a tree
Sat and chanted cheerily
A little song, a pleasant song,
Which was — she sang it all day long —
" When the wind blows the blossoms fall,
But a good God reigns over all."

There passed a lady by the way,
Moaning in the face of day;
There were tears upon her cheek,
Grief in her heart too great to speak;
Her husband died but yester-morn,
And left her in the world forlorn.

She stopped and listened to the child
That looked to heaven, and singing, smiled;
And saw not, for her own despair,
Another lady, young and fair,
Who also passing, stopped to hear
The infant's anthem ringing clear.

For she but few sad days before
Had lost the little babe she bore;
And grief was busy at her soul
As that sweet memory o'er her stole,

And showed how bright had been the Past,
The Present drear and overcast.

And as they stood beneath the tree
Listening, soothed and placidly,
A youth came by, whose sunken eyes
Spake of a load of miseries;
And he, arrested like the twain
Stopped to listen to the strain.

Death had bowed the youthful head
Of his bride beloved, his bride unwed;
Her marriage robes were fitted on,
Her fair young face with blushes shone,
When the destroyer smote her low,
And changed the lover's bliss to woe.

And these three listened to the song,
Silver toned, and sweet, and strong,
Which that child, the livelong day,
Chanted to itself in play —
"When the wind blows the blossoms fall,
But a good God reigns over all."

The widow's lip impulsive moved;
The mother's grief, though unreproved,
Softened, as her trembling tongue
Repeated what the infant sung,

And the sad lover, with a start,
Conned it over to his heart.

And though the child — if child it were,
And not a seraph sitting there —
Was seen no more — the sorrowing three
Went on their way resignedly,
The song still ringing in their ears; —
Was it music of the spheres?

Who shall tell? They did not know;
But in the midst of deepest woe
The strain recurred when sorrow grew,
To warn them and console them too:
"When the wind blows the blossoms fall,
But a good God reigns over all."

ON DEATH.

TRANSLATED FROM AN ANCIENT GERMAN HYMN.

My God! I know too well that I must die; —
I am but man who soon departeth;
I here inherit no propriety
That long and fast abideth.

Now therefore show me graciously,
How I may meet death happily.

My God! I know not when I must
  Away; no moment glides securely.
How soon a potsherd breaketh into dust!
  The flower it fades how easily!
Therefore but ever make me ready
Now in time for my eternity.

My God! I know not how I am to die,
  For death its ways hath variously.
To one there is a bitter sev'rance of life's tie:
  Another passeth off most peacefully.
Still as thou wilt; grant me only this,—
My end may not be reasonless.

My God! I know not where I am to die,
  Nor where 's the sand 'neath which my grave shall lie;
Still let but this my blessed heirship be,
  That thy good Word to life may waken me;
Then take I gladly any clime whatever,
For all the earth is thine in every part whatever.

Now, dearest God! if I indeed must die,
  Then, take thou to thee, take my spirit,
  Christ's blood its only bath and merit.

And have I Jesus only to me nigh,
  Then 'tis all one to my poor heart,
  When, how and where, must I depart.

TRIUMPH IN DEATH.

[Written in the immediate prospect of death, by Richard Langhorn, an English lawyer, who, by means of false witnesses, was unjustly convicted of high treason, and executed during the reign of Charles II.]

It is told me I must die.
O happy news!
Be glad, oh my soul,
And rejoice in Jesus thy Saviour.
If he intended thy perdition,
Would he have laid down his life for thee?
Would he have expected thee with so much patience?
And given thee so long a time for penance?
Would he have called thee with so much love?
And illuminated thee with the light of his Spirit?
Would he have drawn thee with so great force?
And favored thee with so many graces?
Would he have given thee so many good desires?
Would he have set the seal of the predestinate upon thee?

And dressed thee in his own livery?
Would he have given thee his own cross?
And given thee shoulders to bear it with patience?

It is told me I must die.
O happy news!
Come on, my dearest soul.
Behold! thy Jesus calls thee.
He prayed for thee upon his cross;
There he bowed down his head to kiss thee;
There he cried out with a powerful voice,
"Father, receive him, he is mine."
There he opened his heart to give thee entrance;
There he gave up his life to purchase life for thee.

It is told me I must die.
O, happy news!
I shall be freed from misery;
I shall no more suffer pain;
I shall no more be subject to sin;
I shall no more be in danger of being damned.
But from henceforth I shall see, and I shall live;
I shall praise, and I shall bless;
And this I shall always do,
Without ever being weary of doing what I always
aim to do.

It is told me I must die.
O, what happiness!

I am going to the place of my rest;
To the land of the living, to the haven of security;
To the kingdom of peace;
To the palace of my God;
To the nuptial of the Lamb;
To sit at the table of my King, to feed on bread of angels;
To see what no eye hath seen;
To hear what no ear hath heard;
To enjoy what the heart of man cannot comprehend!
O, my Father, thou art the best of all fathers.
Have pity on the most wretched of all thy children.
I was lost, but by thy mercy am now found;
I was dead, but by thy grace am now raised again;
I was gone astray after vanity,
But I am now ready to appear before thee.
O, my father, come now in mercy, and receive thy child;
Give him the kiss of peace;
Remit unto him all his sins;
Clothe him with thy nuptial robe;
Receive him into thy house;
Permit him to have a place at thy feast,
And forgive all those who are guilty of his death.

CHILDLIKE SUBMISSION.

"The cup which my Father hath given me, shall I not drink it?"—John xviii: 11.

Musing of all my Father's love,
(How sweet it is!)
Methought I heard a gentle voice —
"Child, here 's a cup:
I 've mixed it — drink it up."
My heart did sink — I could no more rejoice.

O Father, dost thou love thy child?
Then why this cup?
"One day, my child, I said to thee —
"Here is a flower
Plucked from a beauteous bower:
Did you complain? or take it thankfully?

"One day I gave thee pleasant fruit
From a choice tree:
How pleased, how grateful you did seem:
You said — 'I love
Thee: faithful may I prove!'
Your heart was full; with joy your eyes did beam.

"That flower was mine — that fruit was mine:
This cup is mine,
And all that 's in it comes from me."
Father, I 'm still;

Forgive my naughty will.
But what 's the cup ? --- may I look in and see ?
" *You* see, my child! You must not see —
Christ only saw
His destined cup of bitter gall :
No, child, believe —
Meekly the cup receive,
And know that love and wisdom mixed it all."

O, Father, must it be ?
" Yes, child, it must."
Then give the needed medicine ;
Be by my side —
Only thy face don't hide :
I 'll drink it all — it must be good — 't is Thine.

THE GOOD SHEPHERD.

I was a wandering sheep,
I did not love the fold :
I did not love my Shepherd's voice,
I would not be controled ;
I was a wayward child,
I did not love my home,

I did not love my Father's voice,
  I loved afar to roam.

The Shepherd sought his sheep,
  The Father sought his child;
They followed me o'er vale and hill,
  O'er deserts waste and wild:
They found me nigh to death,
  Famished, and faint, and lone;
They bound me with the bands of love,
  They saved the wandering one!

They spoke in tender love,
  They raised my drooping head;
They gently closed my bleeding wounds,
  My fainting soul they fed;
They washed my filth away,
  They made me clean and fair;
They brought me to my home in peace,
  The long-sought wanderer!

Jesus my Shepherd is,
  'Twas he that loved my soul,
'Twas He that wash'd me in his blood,
  'Twas He that made me whole;
'Twas He that sought the lost,
  That found the wandering sheep,
'Twas He that brought me to the fold,—
  'Tis he that still doth keep.

I was a wandering sheep,
  I would not be controled;
But now I love my Shepherd's voice,
  I love, I love the fold!
I was a wayward child,
  I once preferred to roam,
But now I love my Father's voice, —
  I love, I love his home!

SEVENTH DAY OF CREATION.

Sabbath of the saints of old,
Day of mysteries manifold,
By the great Creator blest,
Type of his eternal rest:
I with thoughts of Thee would seek
To sanctify the closing week.

Resting from his work, the Lord
Spake to-day the hallowing word;
And, his wondrous labors done,
Now the everlasting Son
Gave to heaven and earth the sign
Of a wonder more divine:

Resting from His work, to-day
In the tomb the Saviour lay,
His sacred form from head to feet
Swathed in the winding-sheet,
Lying in the rock alone,
Hid beneath the sealed stone.

All the seventh day long, I ween
Mournful watch'd the Magdalene,
Rising early, resting late,
By the sepulchre to wait,
In the holy garden glade
Where her buried Lord was laid.

So, as closed the Sabbath night,
In Goshen watched the Israelite,
Staff in hand, in pilgrim's guise,
By the slaughtered sacrifice,
Waiting till the midnight cry
Signal gave that God was nigh :

So with Thee till life shall end,
I would solemn vigil spend ;
Let me hew thee, Lord, a shrine,
In this rocky heart of mine,
Where in pure embalmed cell,
None but thee may'st ever dwell.

THE CHURCH PORCH.

HERBERT.

When once thy foot enters the church, be bare :
God is more there than thou ; for thou art there
Only by his permission. Then beware,
And make thyself all reverence and fear.
Kneeling ne'er spoiled silk stockings. Quit thy state,—
All equal are within the church's gate.

Resort to sermons, — but to prayers most :
Prayer is the end of preaching. Oh, be drest!
Stay not for th' other pin. Why, thou hast lost
A joy for it worth worlds. Thus hell doth jest
Away thy blessings, and extremely flout thee ;
Thy clothes being fast, but thy soul loose, about thee.

In time of service seal up both thine eyes,
And send them to thy heart ; that, spying sin,
They may weep out the stains by them did rise —
Those doors being shut, all by the ear comes in.
Who marks, in church time, others' symmetry,
Makes all their beauty his deformity.

Let vain or busy thoughts have there no part :
Bring not thy plough, thy plots, thy pleasures thither ;

Christ purged his temple; so must thou thy heart.
All worldly thoughts are but thieves met together
To cozen thee. Look to thy actions well;
For churches either are our heaven, or hell.

Judge not the preacher; for he is thy judge.
If thou mislike him, thou conceiv'st him not.
God calleth preaching folly. Do not grudge
To pick out treasures from an earthly pot.
The worst speak something good. If *all* want sense,
God takes a text, and preacheth patience.

He that gets patience, and the blessing which
Preachers conclude with, hath not lost his pains;
He that, by being at church, escapes the ditch
Which he might fall in by companions, gains.
He that loves God's abode, and to combine
With saints on earth, shall one day with them shine.

Jest not at preacher's language or expression:
How know'st thou but *thy* sins made him miscarry?
Then turn thy faults and his into confession.
God sent him, whatsoe'r he be. O tarry,
And love him for his Master! His condition,
Though it be ill, makes him no ill physician.

None shall in hell such bitter pangs endure,
As those who mock at God's way of salvation.
Whom oil and balsams kill, what salve can cure?
They drink with greediness a full damnation.
The Jews refus'd thunder, and we folly:
Though God do hedge us in, yet who is holy?

Sum up at night what thou hast done by day;
And in the morning, what thou hast to do.
Dress and undress thy soul. Mark the decay
And growth of it. If, with thy watch, *that* too
Be down, then wind up both. Since we shall be
Most surely judged, make thy accounts agree.

"ABIDE WITH US."

"Abide with us: for it is toward evening, and the day is far spent."—Luke xiv: 29.

Abide with me: fast falls the eventide;
The darkness thickens. Lord, with me abide:
When other helpers fail, and comforts flee,
Help of the helpless, O abide with me!

Swift to its close ebbs out life's little day;
Earth's joys grow dim, its glories pass away:

Change and decay in all around I see;—
O thou who changest not, abide with me.

Not a brief glance I crave, a passing word;
But as thou dwell'st with thy disciples, Lord —
Familiar, condescending, patient, free:
Come not to sojourn, but abide with me.

Come not in terrors, as the King of kings,
But kind and good, with healing in thy wings —
Tears for all woes, a heart for every plea;
Come, Friend of sinners, thus abide with me.

Thou on my head in early youth didst smile,
And though rebellious and perverse meanwhile,
Thou hast not left me, oft as I left thee:
On to the close, O Lord, abide with me.

I need thy presence every passing hour;
What but thy grace can foil the tempter's power?
Who like thyself my guide and stay can be?
Through cloud and sunshine, O abide with me.

I fear no foe, with thee at hand to bless;
Ills have no weight, and tears no bitterness.
Where is Death's sting? Where, Grave, thy victory?
I triumph still, if thou abide with me.

Hold thou thy cross before my closing eyes,
Shine through the gloom, and point me to the skies;
Heaven's morning breaks, and earth's vain shadows flee:
In life, in death, O Lord, remember me.

"COME UP HITHER."—Rev. iv: 1.

[The last clod had been laid upon her grave, and I had returned to the silence and solitude of my desolate home. Alone with bitter thoughts, hour after hour went by, and the first shadows of the coming night began silently to enter the room, where I was sitting in a half trance of grief. Suddenly I became conscious of a presence beside me. Without any manifestation to the outward senses, I felt that SHE was there, yearning towards me with an infinite pity; and the voice which had so long been to me above all other music, sang to my heart the words below.]

I shine in the light of God,
His likeness stamps my brow,
Through the valley of death my feet have trod
And I reign in glory now:
No breaking heart is here,
No keen and thrilling pain,

No wasted cheek, where the frequent tear
  Hath rolled and left its stain.

I have found the joy of heaven,
  I am one of the angel band,
To my head a crown is given,
  And a harp is in my hand.
I have learned the song they sing,
  Whom Jesus hath made free,
And the glorious walls on high shall ring
  With my new-born melody.

No sin — no grief — no pain —
  Safe in my happy home —
My fears all fled — my doubts all slain —
  My hour of triumph come —
O friend of my mortal years!
  The trusted and the tried,
Thou art walking still in the vale of tears,
  But I am by thy side.

Do I forget? Oh no!
  For memory's golden chain
Shall bind my heart to hearts below,
  Till they meet and touch again.
Each link is strong and bright,
  And love's electric flame

Flows freely down like a river of light,
To the world from which I came.

Do you mourn when another star
Shines out from the glittering sky?
Do you weep when the noise of war
And the rage of conflict die?
Then why should your tears roll down,
And your heart be sorely riven,
For another gem in the Saviour's crown,
And another soul in heaven?

"BRING BACK MY FLOWERS."

JUDGE CHARLETON.

A child sat by a limpid stream,
And gazed upon the tide beneath;
Upon her cheek was joy's bright beam,
And on her brow a blooming wreath;
Her lap was filled with blushing flowers,
And as the clear brook babbled by,
She scattered down the rosy showers,
With many a wild and joyous cry,
And laughed to see the mingling tide
Upon the onward progress glide.

And time flew on — and flower by flower
  Was cast upon the sunny stream,
But when the shades of eve did lower,
  She woke up from her blissful dream:
"Bring back my flowers," she wildly cried,
  "Bring back my flowers I flung to thee!"
But echo's voice alone replied,
  As danced the streamlet down the lea:
And still amid night's gloomy hours,
In vain she cried, "Bring back my flowers!"

Oh maiden! who on time's swift stream,
  Most gladly sees thy moments flee,
In this poor child's delusive dream,
  An emblem thou may'st find of thee!
Each moment is a perfumed rose,
  Into thy hand by mercy given,
That thou its fragrance might dispose,
  And let its incense rise to heaven;
Else when death's shadow o'er thee lowers,
Thy heart will wail, "Bring back my flowers!"

THE ABSENT SUN.

Where are thy beams, oh Sun?
The earth stands mourning for thy vanished light,
When will thy rays once more rejoice the sight?

Shine forth again—thou bright and glorious One!
A tinge of gloom is over all things spread,
And nature sighs, and veils her drooping head.

How dark and dim the day!
The stately pines erect their heads on high,
Their sombre foliage mingles with the sky,
A sky as bleak and desolate as they;—
Rock, river, stream and hill wear one dull hue,
And nothing bright or cheerful meets the view.

The Sun—the Sun shines forth!
Now the stream sparkles with a silvery light,
And the blue hills look beautiful and bright;
Again in light and loveliness the earth
Is smiling — all her gloom is chased away,
And joy descends in that reviving ray.

And thus it is with thee,
My soul! how oft a deep and rayless gloom
Hath shrouded thee in darkness like the tomb,
Within, around thee all was dark and sad,
And all in Misery's sombre livery clad.

The Sun returned once more —
The Sun of Righteousness, with healing wings,
He who salvation to the spirit brings;

And all thy darkness and distress were o'er —
Thy Saviour, thy Redeemer smiled, and then
Peace, happiness were made thine own again.

Sun of my soul! oh shine
Forever on my heart — let nought conceal
Thy cheering radiance — let me always feel
Thy warmth, for I am blest while thou art mine;
May no dark clouds of sin and folly rise
To veil thy light from these adoring eyes!

Thy beams shall lead me on
Through all the perils of mine upward way,
Guided by thee my footsteps shall not stray,
And when this earthly pilgrimage is done
I fain would hope that I shall rise above
To Thee, the Fountain-head of Light and Love.

THANKS FOR DAILY BREAD.

ROBERT HERRICK.

Lord, Thou hast given me a cell,
Wherein to dwell;
A little house whose humble roof
Is weather-proof;

Under the spars of which I lie
Both soft and dry;
Where Thou, my chamber for to ward,
Hath set a guard
Of harmless thoughts, to watch and keep
Me while I sleep.
Low is my porch, as is my fate,
Both void of state;
And yet the threshold of my door
Is worn by the poor,
Who hither come, and freely get
Good words or meat.
Like as my parlor, so my hall,
And kitchen small;
A little buttery and therein
A little bin,
Which keeps my little loaf of bread
Unchipt, unflead.
Some little sticks of thorn or brier
Make me a fire,
Close by whose living coal I sit,
And glow like it.
Lord, I confess, too, when I dine,
The pulse is thine,
And all those other bits that be
There placed by thee.
The worts, the purslain, and the mess
Of water cress,

Which of Thy kindness thou has sent:
        And my content
Makes these, and my beloved beet
        To be more sweet.
'Tis Thou that crown'st my glittering hearth
        With guiltless mirth;
And giv'st me wassail bowls to drink,
        Spiced to the brink.
Lord, 'tis thy plenty-dropping hand
        That sows my land;
All this, and better, dost Thou send
        Me, for this end;
That I should render for my part
        A thankful heart,
Which, fired with incense, I resign
        As wholly thine:
But the acceptance — that must be,
        O Lord, by Thee.

PSALM TWENTY-THIRD.

JAMES MERRICK.

Lo, my Shepherd's hand divine!
Want shall never more be mine.
In a pasture fair and large

He shall feed his happy charge,
And my couch with tenderest care,
'Midst the springing grass prepare.
When I faint with summer heat,
He shall lead my weary feet,
To the streams that still and slow
Through the verdant meadow flow.
He my soul anew shall frame,
And, his mercy to proclaim,
When through devious paths I stray
Teach my steps the better way.
Though the dreary vale I tread
By the shades of death o'erspread;
There I walk from terror free,
While my every wish I see
By thy rod and staff supplied;
This my guard and that my guide.
While my foes are gazing on,
Thou thy favoring care hast shown;
Thou my plenteous board hast spread
Thou with oil refreshed my head;
Filled by Thee my cup o'erflows;
For thy Love no limit knows:
Constant to my latest end,
This my footsteps shall attend,
And shall bid thy hallowed Dome
Yield me an eternal home.

JOYFUL THOUGHTS OF DEATH.

["In the Life of Rev. Andrew Fuller, the following hymn is referred to, as being a favorite of that eminent man during the latter pensive years of his life: and especially as being often repeated while paciug his room in the agonies of his last illness."]

I sojourn in a vale of tears,
Alas, how can I sing?
My harp doth on the willows hang,
Dis-tuned in every string.
My music is a captive's-chain;
Harsh sounds my ears do fill;
Nor shall I sing sweet Sion's song,
On this side Sion's hill!

Yet lo! I hear a joyful sound;
"Surely I quickly come!"
Each word much sweetness doth distil,
Like a full honeycomb.
And dost thou come, my dearest Lord?
And dost thou surely come?
And dost thou surely quickly come?
Methinks I am at home.

Come, then, my dearest, dearest Lord,
My sweetest, surest friend;
Come, for I loath these Kedar tents;
Thy fiery chariots send.

What have I here? My thoughts and joys
Are all packed up and gone;
My eager soul would follow them
To thine eternal throne.

What have I in this barren land?
My Jesus is not here;
Mine eyes will ne'er be blest until
My Jesus doth appear.
My Jesus is gone up to heaven,
To get a place for me;
For 'tis his will that where he is
There should his servants be.

Canaan I view from Pisgah's top,
Of Canaan's grapes I taste,
My Lord, who sends unto me here,
Will send for me at last.
I have a God that changeth not,
Why should I be perplexed?
My God that owns me in this world,
Will own me in the next.

Go fearless, then, my soul, with God,
Into another room;
Thou, who hast walked with him here,
Go see thy God at home.

View death with a believing eye;
  It hath an angel's face;
And this kind angel will prefer
  Thee to an angel's place.

The grave seems but a fining pot
  Unto believing eyes;
For there the flesh shall lose its dross,
  And like the sun shall rise.
The world, which I have known so well,
  Hath mocked me with its lies;
How gladly could I leave behind
  Its vexing vanities!

My dearest friends, they dwell above;
  Them will I go and see;
And all my friends in Christ below
  Will soon come after me.
Fear not the trump's earth-rending sound,
  Dread not the day of doom;
For he that is to be thy Judge,
  Thy Saviour is become.

Blest be my God, that gives me light,
  Who in the dark did grope;
Blest be my God, the God of love,
  Who causeth me to hope.

Here the words, signet, comfort, staff,
And here is grace's chain;
By these, thy pledges, Lord, I know,
My hopes are not in vain.

THE SOLITARY WORSHIPPER.

[A single member of the Society of Friends, in Boston, is said to have gone to their place of worship for some years after all his fellow-worshippers were dead.]

Alone and silent there he sat,
Within the house of prayer;
Where once with him his brethren met,
In silent worship there.
They all had gone; the young and old
Were gathered to the dead;
He saw no more their friendly looks,
He heard no more their tread.
Yet still he loved, as came the day,
When they were wont to meet,
To tread the old familiar way,
And take his 'customed seat.
Plain was the place, an humble hall,
In which he sat alone;
The show of forms, the pride of art,

To him were all unknown.
No organ pealed its solemn notes,
No choir the stillness broke,
No preacher read the sacred page,
Or to his hearer spoke;
He needed not these outward things
To wake the reverent mind,
For other ends than such as this
They seemed to him designed.
In silence, gathered to himself,
The Spirit he implored,
And without speech, or outward sign,
The Father he adored.
And to his mind was opened then
The meaning of the word,
"Ask and receive," "seek ye and find,"
The Spirit of the Lord.
That Spirit strengthened and consoled,
And gave him inward sight;
And on his lonely, darkened path
It threw a heavenly light.
No more alone! For he had come
To Zion's holy hill,
The city of the Living God,
That saints and angels fill.
The elders there, with silver locks,
The sisters' modest grace,
The young in all their innocence,

With glory filled the place;
No cloud of sorrow or of care
A soul had ever known,
That in that happy band he saw,
Nor felt he e'er alone.
Their looks of peace, and love unchanged,
Assured his trembling soul;
And bade him banish every fear,
And every doubt control.
With them again, as when on earth,
He held communion sweet;
And, by their sympathy, was made
For heaven's own worship meet.

THE FLOWERS OF GOD.

The welcome flowers are blossoming,
In joyous troops revealed;
They lift their dewy buds and bells,
In garden, mead and field.
They lurk in every sunless path
Where forest-children tread;
They dot, like stars, the sacred turf
Which lies above the dead.

They sport with every playful wind,
  That stirs the blooming trees,
And laugh on every fragrant bush,
  All full of toiling bees.
From the green marge of lake and stream,
  Fresh vale, and mountain sod,
They look in gentle glory forth,
  The pure, sweet flowers of God.

They come, with genial airs and skies,
  In summer's golden prime,
And to the stricken world give back
  Lost Eden's blissful clime:
Outshining Solomon, they come,
  And go full soon away;
But yet, like him, they meekly breathe
  True wisdom while they stay.

"If God," they whisper, "smiles on us
  And bids us bloom and shine,
Does he not mark, O faithless man,
  Each wish and want of thine?
Think, too, what joys await in heaven
  The blest of human birth,
When rapture such as wooes thee now,
  Can reach the bad on earth!"

Redeemer of a fallen race!
  Most merciful of kings!
Thy hallowed words have clothed with power
  These frail and beauteous things;
All taught by thee, they yearly speak
  Their message of deep love,
Bidding us fix, for life and death,
  Our hearts and hopes above.

THE LITTLE COFFIN.

'Twas a tiny, rosewood thing,
Ebon bound, and glittering
With its stars of silver white,
Silver tablet, black and bright,
Downy pillowed, satin lined,
That I, loitering, chanced to find
'Mid the dust and scent and gloom
Of the undertaker's room,
Waiting empty—ah! for whom?

Ah! what love-watched cradle bed
Keeps to-night the nestling head—
Or on what soft, pillowing breast
Is the cherub form at rest,

That ere long, with darkened eye,
Sleeping to no lullaby,
Whitely robed, and still, and cold,
Pale flowers slipping from its hold,
Shall this dainty couch enfold?

Ah! what bitter tears shall stain
All this satin sheet like rain,
And what towering hopes be hid
'Neath this tiny coffin lid,
Scarcely large enough to bear
Little words that must be there,
Little words, cut deep and true,
Bleeding mothers' hearts anew—
Sweet, pet name, and "AGED TWO!"

Oh! can sorrow's hovering plume
Round our pathway cast a gloom,
Chill and darksome as the shade
By an infant's coffin made!
From our arms an angel flies,
And our startled, dazzled eyes,
Weeping round its vacant place,
Cannot rise its path to trace,
Cannot see the angel face!

THE LAW OF THE LIPS.

Speak kindly to thy fellow-man,
Lest he should die, while yet
The bitter accents wring his heart
And make his pale cheek wet.

Speak tenderly to him ; for he
Hath many toils to bear ;
And he is weak, and often sighs—
As thou dost—under care.

Speak lovingly to him ; he is
A brother of thine own :
He well may claim thy sympathies,
Who's bone of thine own bone.

Speak meekly to him ; he may be
A holier man than thou,
And fitting it may be for thee
To him with reverence bow.

Speak solemnly to him ; for thou
And he must surely meet,
To make account for idle words,
Before the judgment-seat.

Speak faithfully to him ; thy word
May touch him deep within,
And save his erring soul from death,
And cover o'er his sin !

MIDNIGHT MUSIC.

MRS. L. H. SIGOURNEY.

["The Rev. Mr. George Herbert, in one of his walks to Salisbury, to join a musical society, saw a poor man with a poorer horse, that had fallen under his load. Putting off his canonical coat, he helped him to unload, and afterwards to load his horse. The poor man blessed him for it, and he blessed the poor man. And so like was he to the good Samaritan, that he gave him money to refresh both himself and his horse, at the same time admonishing him that 'if he loved himself he should be merciful to his beast.'

"So, leaving the poor man, and coming unto his musical friends at Salisbury, they began to wonder, that Mr. George Herbert, who used always to be so trim and clean, should come into that company so soiled and discomposed; but he told them the reason, and one of them said to him, 'he had disparaged himself by so mean an employment,' his answer was, that 'the thought of what he had done would prove *music to him at midnight,* and that the omission of it would have made discord in his conscience, whenever he should pass by that place.' 'For if,' said he, 'I am bound to *pray* for all who are in distress, I am surely bound, as far as it is in my power, to *practice* what I pray for. And though I do not wish for the occasion every day, yet, let me tell you, I would not willingly pass one day of my life, without comforting a sad soul, or showing mercy; and I bless God for this opportunity. So now, let us tune our instruments.'"]

What maketh music when the bird
Doth hush its merry lay,

And the sweet spirit of the flowers
Hath sigh'd itself away?
What maketh music, when the frost
Doth chain the murmuring rill,
And every song that summer woke
In winter's trance is still?

What maketh music, when the winds
To hoarse encounter rise,
When Ocean strikes his thunder-gong
And the rent cloud replies?
When no adventurous planet dares
The midnight arch to deck,
And in its startling dream the babe
Doth clasp its mother's neck?

And when the fiercer storms of life
Do o'er the pilgrim sweep,
And earthquake voices claim the hopes
He treasured long and deep,
When loud the threatening passions roar,
Like lions in their den,
And vengeful tempests lash the shore,—
What maketh music then?

The deed to humble Virtue born,
Which nursing memory taught
To shun the boastful world's applause,
And love the lowly thought,—

This builds a cell within the heart,
Amid the weeds of care,
And tuning high its heaven-strung harp,
Doth make sweet music there.

WILLIE AND THE BIRDS.

A TRUE STORY.

A little black-eyed boy of five
Thus spake to his mamma:
"Do look at all the pretty birds;
How beautiful they are!
How smooth and glossy are their wings —
How beautiful their hue;
Besides, mamma, I really think
That they are PIOUS too."

"Why so, my dear?" the mother said,
And scarce suppressed a smile—
The answer showed a thoughtful head,
A heart quite free from guile;
"Because, when each one bows his head,
His tiny bill to wet,
To lift a thankful glance above,
He never does forget;

And so, mamma, it seems to me,
That very pious they must be."

Dear child, I would a lesson learn
From this sweet thought of thine,
And heavenward, with a glad heart, turn
These earth-bound eyes of mine;
Perfected praise, indeed is given
By babes below, to God in heaven.

THE BURIAL OF MOSES.

"And he buried him in a valley in the land of Moab, over against Bethpeor; but no man knoweth of his sepulchre unto this day.—Deut. xxxiv. 6.

By Nebo's lonely mountain,
On this side Jordan's wave,
In a vale in the land of Moab,
There lies a lonely grave;
And no man dug that sepulchre,
And no man saw it e'er,
For the angels of God upturned the sod,
And laid the dead man there.

That was the grandest funeral
That ever passed on earth;

But no man heard the trampling
  Or saw the train go forth.
Noiselessly as the daylight
  Comes when the night is done,
And the crimson streak on ocean's cheek
  Grows into the great sun;

Noiselessly as the springtime —
  Her crown of verdure weaves,
And all the trees on all the hills
  Open their thousand leaves;
So, without sound of music,
  Or voice of them that wept,
Silently down, from the mountain's crown,
  The great procession swept.

Perchance the bald old eagle,
  On grey Bethpeor's height,
Out of his rocky eirie
  Looked on the wondrous sight.
Perchance the lion stalking
  Still shuns that hallowed spot;
For beast and bird have seen and heard
  That which man knoweth not.

But when the warrior dieth,
  His comrades in the war,
With arms reversed and muffled drum,
  Follow the funeral car:

They show the banners taken,
They tell his battles won,
And after him lead his masterless steed,
While peals the minute gun.

Amid the noblest of the land,
Men lay the sage to rest,
And give the bard an honored place
With costly marble drest.
In the great minster transept,
Where lights like glories fall,
And the sweet choir sings, and the organ rings
Along the emblazoned wall.

This was the bravest warrior
That ever buckled sword;
This the most gifted Poet
That ever breath'd a word;
And never earth's philosopher
Traced with his golden pen
On the deathless page, truths half so sage
As he wrote down for men.

And had he not high honor?
The hill-side for his pall,
To lie in state while angels wait,
With stars for tapers tall,
And the dark rock pines like tossing plumes
Over his bier to wave,

And God's own hand in that lonely land
To lay him in the grave.

In that deep grave without a name,
Whence his uncoffin'd clay
Shall break again, most wondrous thought,
Before the Judgment Day;
And stand with glory wrapped around
On the hills he never trod,
And speak of the strife that won our life
With th' Incarnate Son of God!

O lonely tomb in Moab's land,
O dark Bethpeor's hill,
Speak to these curious hearts of ours,
And teach them to be still!
God hath his mysteries of grace,
Ways that we cannot tell;
He hides them deep, like the secret sleep
Of him he loved so well.

SCRIPTURE AND REASON.

COWLEY.

The holy book, like the eighth sphere doth shine
With thousand lights of truth divine;

So numberless the stars, that to the eye
It makes but all one galaxy.
Yet reason must assist too, for in seas
So vast and dangerous as these,
Our course by stars above we cannot know,
Without the compass too below.
Though reason cannot through faith's mysteries see,
It sees that there and such they be;
Though it, like Moses, by a sad command
Must not come into th' Holy Land,
Yet thither it infallibly does guide,
And from afar 'tis all descried.

CHASTISEMENT.

HERBERT.

What, (many times I musing asked,) is man,
If grief and care
Keep far from him? He knows not what he can,
Or cannot bear.

He, till the fire hath purged him, doth remain
Mixed all with dross;
To lack the loving discipline of pain
Were endless loss;

Yet when my Lord did ask me on what side
I were content,
The grief, whereby I must be purified
To me were sent—

As each imagined anguish did appear,
Each withering bliss
Before my soul, I cried, "O spare me here!
Oh no, — not this!"

Like one that having need of, deep within,
The surgeon's knife,
Would hardly bear that it should graze the skin,
Though for his life.

Nay then, but He who best doth understand
Both what we need,
And what can bear, did take my case in hand,
Nor crying heed.

LEGEND OF SAINT AUGUSTINE.

Along the shore of summer sea,
Walked Saint Augustine thoughtfully;
Too deeply did he seek to scan
The nature of the Lord of man.

Nor was the task abstruse, he thought —
His mind with Scripture texts was fraught;
He deemed to his presumption given
To learn the mysteries of Heaven.

Then suddenly descried he there
A boy of aspect wondrous fair,
Who, bending forward, o'er the strand,
Scooped out a hollow in the sand,
And filled it with a limpid shell,
From out the ocean's briny well.

Augustine spake. "My pretty boy,
What is thy play or thy employ?"
"Look, Sir! within this little hole,
The sea with all the waves that roll
For sport I'll put." Augustine smiled.
"Thy sport is all for naught, my child;
Thy utmost labor is in vain,
Thine aim thou never canst attain." —
"Let him to whom such power's denied,
Content in his own path abide;
Much to the loving heart is dear,
That to the brain doth dark appear." —
So spake the boy: then to the light
His wings displayed, of glistening white,
And like an eagle soared away,
Lost in the sun's resplendent ray.

Long after him Augustine gazed,
And said, with heart and eyes upraised,
"The truth he spake: the human mind
Is still to time and space confined,
And cannot pass beyond; but he
Who lives in faith and righteously,
So much of God shall he discern
As needeth man on earth to learn."

THE CRY OF WANT.

VAUGHAN.

Such is man's life, and such is mine,
The worst of men, and yet still thine;
Still thine! Thou know'st, and if not so
Then give me over to my foe;
Yet since, as easy 'tis for Thee
To make man good, as bid him be,
And with one glance (could he that gain)
To look him out of all his pain,
O send me from Thy holy hill
So much of strength as may fulfil
All thy delights, (whate'er they be)
And sacred institutes in me:
Open my rocky heart, and fill

It with obedience to thy will ;
Then seal it up, that as none see,
So none may enter there but Thee.
O hear, my God! Hear Him whose blood
Speaks more and better for my good!
O let my cry come to thy throne!
My cry not poured with tears alone,
(For tears alone are often foul,)
But with the blood of all my soul,
With spirit sighs, and earnest groans,
Faithful and most repenting moans;
With these I cry, and crying pine,
Till Thou both mend, and make me thine.

THE RAIN DROP.

It fell upon my burning cheek—
  A single drop of rain :
I upward glanced its source to seek,
  But upward glanced in vain.
The sky was clear, the sun was bright,
  No cloud was drifting nigh :
'Twas but one breath of vapor light,
  Condensed as it flew by.

Yet 'twas the self-same Power that made
   And poised this earthly ball,
Which in its flight that vapor stayed,
   And caused its gentle fall.
Nor was it downward sent for nought:
   It broke a dark day-dream,
Dispelled a train of painful thought,
   And woke a noble theme.

I mused on one too fondly loved,
   Too fondly prized and sung,
Who had both cold and faithless proved,
   And had my heart-strings wrung;
That rain-drop raised my downcast eye
   To yon bright vault of blue,
And checked at once the bursting sigh,
   And chased the vision too.

I turned from all the charms of earth,
   From cisterns rent and dry,
To Him who gave the planets birth,
   Yet hears the ravens' cry.
I dwelt on all his wondrous grace
   To lost mankind — to me;
And vowed no idol more to place
   Where He alone should be.

O Lord, accept my contrite vow;
   My carnal thoughts control;

Impress thy signet on my brow,
  Thy likeness on my soul!
Be thou the sovereign of my heart,
  And make that heart thy throne,
Till I shall see Thee as thou art,
  And know Thee as I'm known!

NO EVIL BUT SIN.

Doth sadness in thy soul abide?
  Resume the smile of cheer;
And be Jehovah's will thine own:
The light that shines around the throne
  Shall make his purpose clear.

Naught is an evil, though it lay
  Thy dearest idol low,
Until, contending with the dart,
Thy proud and unsubmissive heart
  Decides to make it so.

Count naught an evil, while the breast
  From self-reproach is free —
Count naught an evil, save the sin
That, coiling dark the soul within,
  Doth hide God's face from thee.

THE DYING CHRISTIAN.

A holy calm was on his brow,
  And peaceful was his breath,
And o'er his pallid features stole
  The trace of coming death.
We asked, "Art ready to depart?"
  He smiled with joy divine,
And spoke the language of his soul,
  "*My Master's time is mine!*

NEARER TO THEE.

Along the mountain-track of life,
  Along the weary lea,
O'er rocks, 'mid storms, in joy, in strife,
  Let this my heart-cry be,
"Nearer to Thee!" "Nearer to Thee!"

This pilgrim-path by Thee was trod,
  Jesus! my King! by Thee!
Traced by Thy feet, Thy tears, Thy blood,
  In love, in death, for me —
O bring my soul nearer to Thee!

Let every step, let every thought,
  Sweet memories bear of Thee!
And hear the soul Thy love hath bought,
  Whose way-cry oft shall be,
"Nearer to Thee! "Nearer to Thee!"

Thou wilt! Thou dost! A small still voice
  Teacheth of faith in Thee;
Of hope, that might in grief rejoice,
  If still the way-cry be,
"Nearer to Thee!" "Nearer to Thee!"

Yet a few days to me, perhaps,
  And time no more shall be:
But boundless love can know no lapse;
  Thou art Eternity!
Draw thou my soul "Nearer to Thee!'

Be it the heaven I hope above,
  To live and move in Thee!
O by thy past, thy promised love,
  Grant these blest words to me,
"Ascend, Forgiven!—Nearer to Thee!"

LITTLE LUCY,

AND THE SONG SHE SUNG.

A little child, six summers old,
So thoughtful and so fair,
There seemed about her pleasant ways
A more than childish air,
Was sitting, on a summer eve,
Beneath a spreading tree,
Intent upon an ancient book,
Which lay upon her knee,
She turned each page with careful hand,
And strained her sight to see,
Until the drowsy shadows slept
Upon the grassy lea;
Then closed the book, and upward looked,
And straight began to sing
A simple verse of hopeful love —
This very childish thing: —
"While here below, how sweet to know
His wondrous love and story,
And then, through grace, to see his face,
And live with him in glory!"

That little child, one dreary night
Of winter wind and storm,
Was tossing on a weary couch
Her weak and wasted form;

And in her pain, and in its pause,
But clasped her hands in prayer —
(Strange that we had no thoughts of heaven,
While hers were only there) —
Until she said, "O mother dear,
How sad you seem to be!
Have you forgotten that He said,
"Let children come to me"?
Dear mother, bring the blessed Book,
Come, mother, let us sing."
And then again, with faltering tongue,
She sung that childish thing:
"While here below, how sweet to know
His wondrous love and story,
And then, through grace, to see his face,
And live with him in glory!"

Underneath a spreading tree
A narrow mound is seen,
Which first was covered by the snow,
Then blossomed into green;
Here first I heard that childish voice
That sings on earth no more;
In heaven it hath a richer tone,
And sweeter than before:
For those who know his love below —
So runs the wondrous story —
In heaven, through grace, shall see his face,
And dwell with him in glory!

PILGRIM SONGS.

REV. W. C. DANA.

"Thy statutes have been my songs in the house of my pilgrimage."—Ps. cxix: 54.

The songs that cheer the pilgrim's way
Who seeks a better home on high,
Purer than any earthly lay,
Sublimely swell, and sweetly die.

They tell of joys unknown to earth,
They tell of raptures yet to come,
In that bright world which gave them birth,
Whose mansions are the pilgrim's home.

And as, when music wakes the strings,
Tho lonely sorrowing exile hears
No strain so sweet as that which brings
The memory of departed years.

So, to the pilgrim exiled long
From that blest home for which he sighs,
The only joy-inspiring song,
Is that which points him to the skies.

And, sometimes, when its murmurs roll,
While pure devotion fills the breast,
And gently gliding to the soul,
They hush all earthly cares to rest.

There comes a soft, responsive note,
  A strain like that which angels sing—
It comes from regions far remote,
  And all around its echoes ring.

That strain is not of earth; 'tis given
  To cheer the pilgrim's heart alone:
It is the melody of heaven;
  It echoes from th' eternal throne.

With transport that no tongue can tell,
  He hears that song of rapture high
In strains of sacred grandeur swell,
  In tones of melting sweetness die.

O pilgrim, catch the heavenly strain,
  And waken to its lingering thrills,
Till earth no more thy soul enchain,
  Till joys sublime thy bosom fill.

Nor shalt thou be an exile long;
  Even now bright angels bid thee come,
To join in that eternal song,
  To rest in thy eternal home.

GOOD NIGHT.

CHARLES THE FIRST.

Close thine eyes and sleep secure,
Thy soul is safe — thy body sure;
He that guards thee — He that keeps
Never slumbers — never sleeps.
A quiet conscience in the breast
Has only peace — has only rest.
The music and the mirth of kings
Are out of tune unless *she* sings.
Then close thine eyes in peace, and sleep secure;
No sleep so sweet as thine — no rest so sure.

THE WISH AND THE PRAYER.

BY ELLWOOD, THE FRIEND OF MILTON.

O that mine eye might closed be,
To what becomes me not to see;
That deafness might possess mine ear,
To what concerns me not to hear;
That truth my tongue might always tie,
From ever speaking foolishly!
That no vain thought might ever rest,
Or be conceived within my breast;

That by each word, each deed, each thought
Glory may to my God be brought;
But what are wishes? Lord, mine eye
On thee is fixed; to thee I cry.
O, purge out all my dross, my sin,
Make me more white than snow within;
Wash, Lord, and purify my heart,
And make it clean in every part;
And when 'tis clean, Lord, keep it so,
For that is more than I can do.

BLESSED BE THY NAME.

HOGG.

Blessed be Thy name forever,
Thou of life the guard and giver;
Thou canst guard thy creatures sleeping,
Heal the heart long broke with weeping:
God of stillness and of motion,
Of the desert and the ocean,
Of the mountain, rock, and river,
Blessed be Thy name forever!

Thou who slumberest not, nor sleepest,
Blest are they thou kindly keepest;

God of evening's parting ray,
Of midnight's gloom, and dawning day,
That rises from the azure sea,
Like breathings of eternity;
God of life! that fade shall never,
Blessed be Thy name forever!

THE BLESSING.

I was within a house of prayer,
And many a wounded heart was there;
And many an aching heart was bowed,
Humbly amidst the kneeling crowd:
Nor marvel; — where earth's children press
There must be thought of bitterness.

Oh! in the change of human life —
The anxious wish, the toil, the strife —
How much we know of grief and pain,
Ere one short week comes round again.
Bend every knee, lift every heart;
We need God's blessing ere we part.

Then sweetly through the hallowed bound
Woke the calm voice of solemn sound;

And gladly many a listening ear
Watched that pure tone of love to hear:
And on each humbled heart and true,
GOD'S holy blessing fell like dew.

Like dew on Summer's thirsty flowers;
On the mown grass like softest showers;
On the parched earth like blessed rain,
That calls the Spring bloom back again!
Oh! to how many a varied sigh
Did that sweet benison reply!

"The peace that God bestows,
Through Him who died and rose;
The peace the FATHER giveth through the SON
Be known in every mind,
The broken heart to bind,
And bless ye travellers as ye journey on.

"Ere this week's strife begin,
The war without, within;
The TRIUNE GOD with spirit and with power,
Now on each bended head
His wondrous blessing shed,
And keep you all, through every troubled hour!"

And then within the holy place
Was silence for a minute's space;

Such silence, that you seemed to hear
The holy Dove's wings hovering near;
And the still blessing far and wide,
Tell like the dew at evening tide;
And ere we left the house of prayer,
We knew that peace descended there;
And through the week of strife and din,
We bore its wondrous seal within!

THE SHEPHERD.

Suggested by an allegory of Bishop Heber's, and written by the dying bed of one of the lambs of the Saviour's flock.

There was an eastern shepherd,
Who had a lovely child,
The dearest and the fondest
On which that parent smiled.

But bitter winds came sweeping;
The tender stem gave way,
Its early buds were scattered
In premature decay.

The father sat in silence
And sorrow by his side,

His spirit was in bitterness,
 And peevishly he cried:

"Oh! it was cruel, cruel,
 To call thee thus away:
That what I loved so fondly,
 Might here no longer stay.

"I could have spared another,
 Though with a deep-drawn sigh;
But thou,— my heart's best treasure,—
 I thought not *thou* couldst die."

Yet quickly was he silenced,
 For when he raised his eye,
A stranger mild and courteous
 Was standing watching by.

Not a single word was spoken,
 For the stranger did not stay,
But raised his hand in silence,
 And beckoned him away.

'Twas the solemn hour of midnight,
 The moon was shining bright,
And every thing around them
 Wrapped in its silvery light.

They passed each varied object
  In saddened silence by;
Till they came unto the fold
  Where sheep slept quietly.

"I am a shepherd too," (he said,)
  "With a better fold than thine,
With pastures green and waters clear,
  And skies that ever shine.

"Now, if *thou* wert to take a lamb
  To fondle to *thy* breast,
Wouldst thou not choose the youngest one,
  The loveliest and the best?

"Then, wherefore grieve that when I came
  To take a lamb from *thee*,
I chose the fairest of the flock
  To come and dwell with me?"

The stranger paused,—the father turned,
  And raised his tearful eye;
He stood *alone* in the starlit fold,
  Where the sheep slept quietly.

He threw him down on the dewy grass,
  And strove a *prayer* to raise;
But his voice was lost in *thankfulness*,
  And his heart was filled with *praise*.

GOD KNOWS IT ALL.

In the dim recess of thy spirit's chamber,
Is there some hidden grief thou may'st not tell?
Let not thy heart forsake thee; but remember,
His pitying eye, who sees and knows it well.
God knows it all!

And art thou tossed on billows of temptation,
And would'st do good, but evil oft prevails?
O think amid the waves of tribulation
When earthly hopes, and earthly refuge fails—
God knows it all!

And dost thou sin, thy deed of shame concealing
In some dark spot no human eye can see,
Then walk in pride, without one sigh revealing
The deep remorse that should disquiet thee?
God knows it all!

Art thou oppressed, and poor, and heavy hearted,
The heavens above thee in thick clouds arrayed,
And well nigh crushed; no earthly thought imparted,
No friendly voice to say, "Be not afraid!"
God knows it all!

Art thou a mourner? are thy tear-drops flowing
For one too early lost to earth and thee?

The depths of grief no human spirit knowing,
  Which moan in secret, like the moaning sea?
                    God knows it all!

Dost thou look back upon a life of sinning?
  Forward, and tremble for thy future lot?
There's One who sees the end from the beginning,
  Thy tear of penitence is unforgot —
                    God knows it all!

Then go to God. Pour out your hearts before him;
  There is no grief your Father cannot feel;
And let your grateful songs of praise adore him—
  To save, forgive, and every wound to heal.
            God knows it all—God knows it all!

"I WOULD NOT LIVE ALWAY."

"I would not live alway" — but here I would stay,
Till thou, O my Saviour, shalt call me away;
In faith and in hope looking upward to Thee,
Who art pardon, and peace, and salvation to me.

"I would not live alway"— but sweet are the days
Which here I may spend in devotion and praise,—

Days blest with the presence and cheered with the
love
Of Him who will lead me to glory above.

"I would not live alway"—but Thy blessed will
While I live, O my God, let me gladly fulfil,
And seek by obedience true and sincere,
Thy great name to honor and glorify here.

"I would not live alway"—but dwelling below,
Where sin has occasioned such wide-spreading wo,
Let me seek the sad heart of the mourner to cheer,
To comfort and bless the afflicted ones here.

"I would not live alway"—but here let me seek
The guilty to warn, and to strengthen the weak;
To point the lost soul to a Saviour above,
Who waits to receive him with tenderest love.

"I would not live always"—but while I remain,
Let me welcome alike every pleasure and pain
Which proceeds from His hand who is faithful and
true,
Who in mercy chastises and pities me too.

"I would not live alway"—whenever Thy voice,
Redeemer! shall call me, my soul shall rejoice;

Then, saved by thy grace, may I gladly arise
To meet thee, and dwell with thee, Lord, in the skies!

ABIDE IN ME AND I IN YOU.

That mystic word of thine, oh Sovereign Lord!
Is all too pure, too high, too deep for me;
Weary of striving, and with longing faint,
I breathe it back again in prayer to thee.

Abide in me, I pray, and I in thee,
From this good hour. O leave me never more;
Then shall the discord cease, the wound be healed,
The life-long bleeding of the soul be o'er.

Abide in me — o'ershadowed by thy love,
Each half-formed purpose and dark thought of sin;
Quench, ere it rise, each selfish low desire,
And keep my soul as thine calm and divine.

As some rare perfume in a vase of clay
Pervades it with a fragrance not its own —
So when thou dwellest in a mortal soul,

All heaven's own sweetness seems around it
thrown.

The soul alone, like a neglected harp,
Grows out of tune, and needs that hand divine;
Dwell thou within it, tune and touch the chords,
Till every note and string shall answer thine.

Abide in me; there have been moments pure
When I have seen thy face and felt thy power;
Then evil lost its grasp, and passion hushed
Owned the divine enchantment of the hour.

These were but seasons beautiful and rare;
Abide in me — and they shall ever be;
I pray thee now fulfil my earnest prayer —
Come and abide in me, and I in Thee.

LITTLE AT FIRST, BUT MIGHTY AT LAST.

CHARLES MACKAY.

A traveller through a dusty road
Strewed acorns on the lea,
And one took root and sprouted up,

And grew into a tree.
Love sought its shade at evening time
To breathe its early vows,
And Age was pleased, in heats of noon,
To bask beneath its boughs;
The dormouse loved its dangling twigs,
The birds sweet music bore,
It stood a glory in its place,
A blessing evermore!

A little spring had lost its way
Among the grass and fern;
A passing stranger scooped a well,
Where weary men might turn.
He walled it in, and hung with care
A ladle at the brink —
He thought not of the deed he did,
But judged that toil might drink.
He passed again, — and lo, the well,
By summers never dried,
Had cooled ten thousand parching tongues,
And saved a life beside.

A dreamer dropped a random thought;
'Twas old, and yet 'twas new —
A simple fancy of the brain,
But strong in being true.
It shone upon a genial mind,

And lo! its light became
A lamp of life, a beacon ray,
A monitory flame.
The thought was small — its issue great;
A watch-fire on the hill,
It shed its radiance far adown,
And cheers the valley still!

A nameless man, amid a crowd
That thronged the daily mart,
Let fall the word of hope and love,
Unstudied from the heart;
A whisper on the tumult thrown —
A transitory breath —
It raised a brother from the dust,
It saved a soul from death.
O germ! O fount! O word of Love!
O thought at random cast!
Ye were but little at the first,
Yet mighty at the last!

ONLY ONE LIFE.

'Tis not for man to trifle! life is brief
And sin is here.

Our age is but the falling of a leaf,
A dropping tear.
We have no time to sport away the hours:
All must be earnest in a world like ours.

Not many lives, but only one have we,—
One, only one;—
How sacred should that one life ever be,—
That narrow span! —
Day after day filled up with blessed toil,
Hour after hour still bringing in new spoil.

HYMN FOR AN INFANT CLASS.

A giddy lamb one afternoon
Had from the fold departed;
The tender shepherd missed it soon,
And sought it broken-hearted.
Not all the flocks that shared his love
Could from the search delay him,
Nor clouds of midnight darkness move,
Nor fear of suffering stay him.

But night and day he went his way
In sorrow, till he found it;

And when he saw it fainting lie,
He clasped his arms around it.
Then, safely folded to his breast,
From every ill to save it,
He brought it to his home of rest,
And pitied and forgave it.

And thus the Saviour will receive
The little ones who fear him;
Their pains remove, their sins forgive,
And draw them gently near him.
Bless while they live, and when they die,
When flesh and spirit sever —
Conduct them to his throne on high,
To dwell with him forever.

OUR REST.

"The sufferings of this present time are not worthy to be compared with the glory which shall be revealed in us." — [Rom. viii: 18.

My feet are worn and weary with the march
O'er the rough road, and up the steep hill-side;
Oh! city of our God, I fain would see
Thy pastures green, where peaceful waters glide.

My hands are weary too, with toiling on,
  Day after day for perishable meat;
Oh! city of our God, I fain would rest—
  I sigh to gain thy glorious mercy-seat.

My garments, travel-worn and stained with dust,
  Oft rent by briars and thorns that crowd my way,
Would fain be made, O Lord, my righteousness,
  Spotless and white in Heaven's unclouded ray.

My eyes are weary looking at the sin,
  Impiety and scorn upon the earth;
Oh! city of our God, within thy walls
  All—all are clothed again with thy new birth.

My heart is weary of its own deep sin—
  Sinning, repenting, sinning still again;
When shall my soul thy glorious presence feel,
  And find, dear Saviour, it is free from stain?

Patience, poor soul, the Saviour's feet were worn;
  The Saviour's heart and hands were weary, too;
His garments stained, and travel-worn, and old;
  His vision blinded with a pitying dew.

Love thou the path of sorrow that he trod;
  Toil on, and wait in patience for thy rest;
Oh! city of our God, we soon shall see
  Thy glorious walls—home of the loved and blest.

WATCH, WATCH, MOTHER.

Mother! watch the little feet
  Climbing o'er the garden wall,
Bounding through the busy street,
  Ranging cellar, shed and hall;
Never count the moments lost,
Never mind the time it cost;
Little feet will go astray,
Guide them, mother, while you may.

Mother! watch the little hand
  Picking berries by the way,
Making houses in the sand,
  Tossing on the fragrant hay.
Never dare the question ask,
"Why to me this weary task?"
These same little hands may prove
Messengers of light and love.

Mother! watch the little tongue
  Prattling eloquent and wild,
What is said, and what is sung,
  By the happy, joyous child.
Catch the word while yet unspoken,
Stop the vow before 'tis broken;
This same tongue may yet proclaim
Blessings in a Saviour's name.

Mother! watch the little heart
  Beating soft and warm for you;
Wholesome lessons now impart;
  Keep, O! keep that young heart true;
Extricating every weed,
Sowing good and precious seed,
Harvest rich you then may see
Ripening for eternity.

THE MOTHERLESS.

MRS. WELBY.

Thou art not mine — upon thy sweet lips linger
    Thy mothers smile —
And while I press thy soft and baby fingers
    In mine the while —
In the deep eyes, so trustfully upraising
    Their light to mine —
I deem the spirit of thy mother gazing
    To my soul's shrine.
They ask me, with their meek and soft beseeching,
    A mother's care —
They ask a mother's kind and patient teaching —
    A mother's prayer; —
Not mine — yet dear to me—fair fragrant blossom

Of a fair tree —
Crush'd to the earth in life's first glorious summer—
Thou'rt dear to me.
Child of the lost, the buried, and the sainted,
I call thee mine —
Till fairer still, with tears and sin untainted —
Her home be thine.

FAITH.

Ye who think the truth ye sow
Lost beneath the winter's snow,
Doubt not, Time's unerring law
Yet shall bring the genial thaw.
God in Nature ye can trust;
Is the God of Mind less just?

Read we not the mighty thought
Once by ancient sages taught?
Though it withered in the blight
Of the mediæval night,
Now the harvest we behold;
See! it bears a thousand fold.

Workers on the barren soil,
Yours may seem a thankless toil;

Sick at heart with hope deferred,
Listen to the cheering word:
Now the faithful sower grieves;
Soon he'll bind his golden sheaves.

If Great Wisdom have decreed
Man must labor, yet the seed
Never in this life shall grow,
Shall the sower cease to sow?
The fairest fruit may yet be borne
On the resurrection morn.

THE SOWER TO HIS SEED.

FROM THE GERMAN.

Sink, little seed, in the earth's black mould,
Sink in your grave so wet and so cold —
    There must you lie;
  Earth I throw over you,
  Darkness must cover you,
    Light comes not nigh.

What grief you'd tell, if words you could say!
What grief make known for loss of the day!
    Sadly you'd speak:

"Lie here must I ever?
Will the sunlight never
My dark grave seek?"

Have faith, little seed; soon yet again
Thoul't rise from the grave where thou art lain
Thoul't be so fair,
With thy green shades so light,
And thy flowers so bright,
Waving in air.

So must we sink in the earth's black mould;
Sink in the grave so wet and so cold;
There must we stay;
Till at last we shall see
Time turn to eternity,
Darkness to day.

DELIGHT IN GOD ONLY.

FRANCIS QUARLES.

I love (and have some cause to love) the earth;
She is my Maker's creature; therefore good:
She is my mother, for she gave me birth;
She is my tender nurse — she gives me food;

But what's a creature, Lord, compared to thee?
Or what's my mother, or my nurse to me?

I love the air; — her dainty sweets refresh
  My drooping soul, and to new sweets invite me;
Her shrill-mouth'd choir sustains me with their
    flesh,
  And with their polyphonian notes delight me:
But what's the air or all the sweets that she
Can bless my soul withal, compared to Thee?

I love the sea: she is my fellow-creature,
  My careful purveyor: she provides me store;
She walls me round; she makes my diet greater;
  She wafts my treasure from a foreign shore:
But, Lord of oceans, when compared with thee,
What is the ocean, or her wealth to me?

To heaven's high city I direct my journey,
  Whose spangled suburbs entertain mine eye;
Mine eye, by contemplation's great attorney,
  Transcends the crystal pavement of the sky:
But what is heaven, great God, compared to thee?
Without thy presence heaven's no heaven to me.

Without thy presence earth gives no refection;
  Without thy presence, sea affords no treasure;
Without thy presence, air's a rank infection;

Without thy presence, heaven itself no pleasure:
If not possessed, if not enjoyed in thee,
What's earth, or sea, or air, or heaven to me?

The highest honors that the world can boast,
Are subjects far too low for my desire;
The brightest beams of glory are, at most,
But dying sparkles of thy living fire:
The loudest flames that earth can kindle, be
But nightly glow-worms, if compared to thee.

Without thy presence, wealth is bags of cares;
Wisdom but folly; joy, disquiet — sadness:
Friendship is treason, and delights are snares;
Pleasures but pain, and mirth but pleasing madness.
Without thee, Lord, things be not what they be,
Nor have they being, when compared with thee.

In having all things, and not thee, what have I?
Not having thee, what have my labors got?
Let me enjoy but thee, what further crave I?
And having thee alone, what have I not?
I wish nor sea, nor land; nor would I be
Possessed of heaven, heaven unpossessed of thee.

THE BORDER LANDS.

Father, into thy loving hands,
My feeble spirit I commit,
While wandering in these border lands,
Until thy voice shall summon it.

Father, I would not dare to choose
A longer life, an earlier death;
I know not what my soul might lose
By shortened or protracted breath.

These border lands are calm and still,
And solemn are their silent shades;
And my heart welcomes them until
The light of life's long evening fades.

I heard them spoken of with dread,
As fearful and unquiet places;
Shades where the living and the dead,
Look sadly in each other's faces.

But since thy hand hath led me here,
And I have seen the border land;
Seen the dark river flowing near,
Stood on the brink as now I stand;

There has been nothing to alarm
My trembling soul: how could I fear,

While thus encircled with thine arm?
  I never felt thee half so near.

What should appal me in a place
  That brings me hourly nearer thee?
When I may almost see thy face —
  Surely 'tis here my soul would be.

They say the waves are dark and deep,
  That faith has perished in the river;
They speak of death with fear, and weep.
  Shall my soul perish? Never, never.

I know that thou wilt never leave
  The soul that trembles while it clings
To thee; I know thou wilt achieve
  Its passage on thine outstretched wings.

And since I first was brought so near
  The stream that flows to the Dead Sea,
I think that it has grown more clear
  And shallow than it used to be.

I cannot see the golden gate
  *Unfolding yet to welcome me;
I cannot yet anticipate
  The joy of heaven's jubilee.

*To my unspeakable sorrow the completing stanza is missing; yet I cannot persuade myself to withdraw the piece. C.

THE ANGEL OF PATIENCE.

A FREE PARAPHRASE OF THE GERMAN.

To weary hearts, to mourning homes,
God's meekest Angel gently comes;
No power has he to banish pain,
Or give us back our lost again;
And yet, in tenderest love, our dear
And Heavenly Father sends him here.

There's quiet in that Angel's glance,
There's rest in his still countenance;
He mocks no grief with idle cheer,
Nor wounds with words the mourner's ear;
But ills and woes he may not cure,
He kindly teaches to endure.

Angel of Patience! sent to calm
Our feverish brow with cooling balm;
To lay the storms of hope and fear,
And reconcile life's smile and tear;
And throbs of wounded pride to still,
And make our own our Father's will!

O thou who mournest on thy way,
With longings for the close of day,
He walks with thee, that Angel kind,
And gently whispers, "Be resigned!
Bear up, bear on — the end shall tell
The dear Lord ordereth all things well!"

LOVE OF GOD.

DALE.

Oh! never, never canst thou know
  What then for thee the Saviour bore;
The pangs of that mysterious woe
  Which wrung his frame at every pore;
The weight that pressed upon his brow,
  The fever of his bosom's core!

Yes! man for man, perchance may brave
The horrors of the yawning grave;
And friend for friend, or child for sire,
Undaunted and unmoved, expire.
From love, or piety, or pride;
But who can die as Jesus died?

A sweet but solitary beam,
  An emanation from above,
Glimmers o'er life's uncertain dream —
  We hail that beam, and call it love!
But fainter than the pale star's ray
Before the noontide blaze of day,
And lighter than the viewless sand
Beneath the waves that sweep the strand
Is all of love that man can know —
All that in angel-breasts can glow —
Compared, O Lord of Hosts, with thine,

Eternal — fathomless — divine!
That love, whose praise, with quenchless fire,
Inflames the blest seraphic choir,
Where perfect rapture reigns above,
And all is love — for THOU art LOVE!

SECRET GRIEF.

The heart knoweth its own bitterness. — [Prov. xiv; 10

A strange power hath the human heart,
By heaven in mercy given;
Strength to perform its wonted part,
While silently 'tis riven;
To smile e'en when each tender string
Is broken one by one,
Hope to the fainting breast to bring,
While in our own, lives none.

To sit beside the sufferer's bed,
And dry the falling tear,
To gently hold the sinking head
And chase away each fear;
To gaze upon the trembling form
Till the lone heart seems broken,

And yet amid the fearful storm,
  To give of grief no token.

To hear that voice, whose slightest tone
  Hath sweetest music been,
Grow weaker, fainter, till each moan
  The listening ear drinks in;
Yet still unmoved, with placid brow
  To meet that languid eye,
Nor show the parting spirit now
  How gladly we would die.

To shut within the blighted heart
  The agony and strife,
And meekly bear our destined part
  Amid the scenes of life;
Nor cast around our own loved throng
  The gloom that reigneth there,
To check the smile, the cheerful sun,
  To cloud their world so fair.

But oh! the soul could never bear
  This weight of silent grief,
Did not its woes one bosom share,
  One, kindly bring relief;
One, who to sympathise, to cheer,
  The path of sorrow trod,

One to the suffering ever near; —
'Tis thine, O Son of God!

'Tis thine to bind the bleeding heart,
To calm the troubled breast,
Strength, hope and heavenly peace impart —
To give the weary rest;
To point beyond this world of pain,
To that bright home above,
Where those who part may meet again,
Joined in unfading love.

THE PRISM.

A leisure moment idly to beguile,
I took a prism; and, with a careless eye,
Sought for the beauteous colors that do lie
Tombed in that glassy shrine; but for awhile
I sought in vain, till, with a conscious smile,
I turned me to the light; then a sunbeam
Glanced swiftly through, dissolving in a stream
Of softened splendor, like an angel's smile.
Spirit of Light and Life! thy Sacred Book
Stands open to my gaze; but oft in vain,
With dull incurious eye, thereon I look,

And all is dark: I turn to Thee again; —
Pour forth thy glorious beams, then shall I learn
to trace
My Father's sovereign love, my Saviour's matchless grace.

THE SHIP AT SEA.

A white sail gleaming on the flood,
And the bright orbed sun on high,
Are all that break the solitude
Of the circling sea and sky;
Nor cloud nor cape is imaged there
Nor isle of ocean, nor of air.

Led by the magnet o'er the tides,
That bark her path explores, —
Sure as unerring instinct guides
The bird to unseen shores:
With wings that o'er the waves expand,
She wanders to a viewless land.

Yet not alone; on ocean's breast,
Though no green islet glows,
No sweet, refreshing spot of rest,

Where fancy may repose;
Nor rock, nor hill, nor tower, nor tree,
Breaks the blank solitude of the sea; —

O not alone! — her beauteous shade
Attends her noiseless way;
As some sweet memory undecayed,
Clings to the heart for aye,
And haunts it, wheresoe'er we go,
Through every scene of joy and woe.

And not alone, for day and night
Escort her o'er the deep;
And round her solitary flight
The stars their vigils keep.
Above, below, are circling skies,
And heaven around her pathway lies.

And not alone, for hopes and fears
Go with her wandering sail;
And bright eyes watch through gathering tears,
Its distant cloud to hail;
And prayers for her at midnight lone
Ascend, unheard by all, save One.

And not alone, for round her, glow
The vital light and air;
And something that in whispers low

Tells to man's spirit there,
Upon her waste and weary road,
A present, all-pervading God!

"I NEVER LOOKED BEHIND."

On Filey Bridge I sat alone,
Upon a summer's day,
Till on that long, dark ridge of stone
The light of evening lay:
And there was silence all arouud,
But for the sea-bird's cry,
And waves that told with warning sound,
The flowing tide was nigh.
They struck, and struck, with solemn shock,
Each louder than the last,
As on the lonely bridge of rock,
The sea was rising fast.

Onward with life's advancing years,
Returning birth-days come,
Telling to man's unwilling ears
That this is not his home.
"Arise ye and depart," it cries—
That voice recurring still;

Joyful to those by Heaven made wise, —
   Bright hopes their bosoms fill.

The waves were breaking all in foam,
   In the dark northern bay;
The south, between me and my home,
   Smooth as a mirror lay.
And sunset hues were gleaming bright,
   Over the rising sea;
So days of age, in heavenly light,
   May sweet and placid be.

A little lass, in wild attire,
   In russet cloak and hood,
Came onward, softly creeping nigher,
   Till by my side she stood;
And then she said, "It's time to go,
   The tide will soon be here."
Homeward we traced our pathway slow,
   The sea still flowing near.
She had a basket on her arm;
   To gather bait she went; —
A little child — she feared no harm,
   There, by her father sent.

Yet, "Once," she said, "too long I staid,
   And high the waters grew."
"What then?" "O! I was not afraid,

I thought my father knew.
I thought my father saw me there,
Would send a boat from shore;—
But it grew dark—I did not dare
To stay there any more.
I sought the cliff where oft I knew
Rabbits run up on high,
And the sheep climbed, and heifers too;
And so, I thought, might I."
"Were you not frightened then, to pass,
So steep a way to find?"
"Oh, no," replied the little lass,
"*I never looked behind.*"

And such, I thought, should Christians be,
In danger not afraid,
Trusting their Father's eye to see,
Their Father's hand to aid.
And when he bids them climb the hill,
And leads them to their home,
Then let them say, obedient still,
"Father, to Thee I come;"
Nor "look behind" on evil past,
But upward, onward, gaze;
And not a glance be downward cast
O'er earth's dark, dreary ways.

There is a Rock that safety gives
To all that seek its side;

The Lord of Life, to all that lives,
  Saviour, and Friend, and Guide.
O seek him then, when storms arise,
  And pathless wilds affright,
While evening darkens in the skies,—
  He is the way, the light.

THE DEATH OF A CHILD.

Ah! not for thee was woven
  That wreath of joy and woe,
That crown of thorns and flowers
  Which all must wear below.
We bend in sadness o'er thee,
  Yet feel that thou art blest,
Loved one! so early summoned
  To enter into rest.

E'en now thy bright young spirit
  From earthly life is free;
Now hast thou met thy Saviour,
  Who smiled on such as thee.
E'en now thou art rejoicing,
  Unsullied as thou art,

In the blest vision promised
  Unto the pure in heart.

Thou Father of our spirits,
  We can but look to thee;
Though chastened, not forsaken
  Shall we thy children be.
We take the cup of sorrow
  As did thy blessed Son;
Teach us to say with Jesus,
  "Thy will, not ours, be done."

ON THE DEATH OF MR. G. K. POMROY.

G. W. BLAGDEN.

Softly sleep in death's cold slumber,
  Thou whose form we oft have seen,
Quickly passed, and few in number,
  Have thy days of suffering been.
      Rest thee, sweetly,
  Rest from sorrow, toil and sin.

Though we linger o'er thee weeping,
  Though that form no more we see—
He who wept o'er Lazarus sleeping,

He who set that sleeper free,
Slumbering Christian,
He shall still remember thee.

Why then mourn we, broken hearted,
Why thus linger o'er thy clay?
All that warmed it has departed,
It is now in endless day;
Happy spirit,
On thy Saviour's bosom lay.

Though no more thy voice of feeling
Shall our cold affections move,
Hark! I hear its echoes stealing,
'Mid the glorious courts above,
Sweetly singing
Wonders of redeeming love.

If departed spirits hover
O'er this world of sin and night,
Spirit of our sainted brother,
Spirit, now so pure and bright,
Hover o'er us,
Hear us ere thou take thy flight.

CONSOLATION.

FOUQUE, AUTHOR OF UNDINE.

When, through Life's avenue so dark and cold,
Downward, and ever down, thy steps are tending,
Behold,
Hope's gentle accents cheer us in descending —
"Ah, be not sad! ah, do not weep!
Ere thou lay thee down to sleep
The sleep of death,
Thou shalt feel anew, Spring's kindly dew,
And the May wind's fragrant breath."

So didst thou speak, dear voice; so didst thou dream!
The brightness of Life's wave hath ebbed away!
A gleam
Of light shines feebly on my darksome way,
But 'tis across the grave so chill!
Cheat me no more — Endure I will
As best I can;
Suffer and fight, and strive with might,
Even as becomes a man.

I am companioned by mine own sweet strain,
Like a clear-shining lamp to light my feet;
Again
Echoing through German bosoms, strong but sweet,

It cheers my spirit's lonely way:
Ah, yes, and I can pray, can pray
Rejoicingly!
For my misdeeds if Jesus pleads,
Who then condemneth me?

ONE REASON FOR LIFE'S SORROWS.

FOUQUE.

If life were fair around thee,
Fair as the heart had willed,
Without a grief to wound thee,
Or a bright hope unfulfilled, —

Mortal, for death preparing,
Could'st thou to death submit?
Thou would'st refuse, despairing,
A world so dear to quit.

But, one by one, thou knowest
Life's gentle bands are riven,
So, cheered at heart, thou goest
Through the deep grave to heaven.

The chains of fear are broken,
Hope's star is bright aloft:
Oft has this truth been spoken,
But never yet too oft.

GOD IS LOVE.

I cannot always trace the way
  Where Thou, Almighty One! dost move;
But I can always, always say
  That God is love.

When fear her chilling mantle flings
  O'er earth, my soul to heaven above,
As to her sanctuary springs,
  For God is love.

When mystery clouds my darkened path,
  I'll check my dread, my doubts reprove;
In this my soul sweet comfort hath,
  That God is love.

Yes, God is love; — a thought like this
  Can every gloomier thought remove,
And turn all tears, all woes to bliss —
  For God is love.

A REAL OCCURRENCE IN A CIRCLE OF FRIENDS.

EDMESTON.

Which is the happiest death to die?
  "Oh," said one, "if I might choose,

Long at the gate of bliss would I lie,
And feast my spirit ere it fly,
With bright, celestial views.
Mine were a lingering death, without pain,
A death which all might love to see,
And mark how bright and sweet should be
The victory I should gain.
Fain would I catch a hymn of love
From the angel harps which ring above,
And sing it, as my parting breath
Quivered and expired in death;—
So that those on earth might hear
The harp-note of another sphere,
And mark, when nature faints and dies,
What springs of heavenly life arise,
And gather from the death they view,
A ray of hope to light them through,
When they should be departing too."

"No," said another, "so not I:
Sudden as thought is the death I would die,
I would suddenly lay my shackles by,
Nor bear a single pang at parting,
Nor see the tear of sorrow starting,
Nor hear the quivering lips that bless me,
Nor feel the hands of love that press me;—
Nor the frame, with mortal terror shaking,
Nor the heart, where love's soft bands are breaking;—

So would I die.
All bliss, without a pang to cloud it,
All joy, without a pain to shroud it; —
Not slain, but caught up, as it were,
To meet my Saviour in the air.
So would I die; —
Oh, how bright,
Were the realms of light,
Bursting at once upon the sight:
Even so
I long to go; —
These parting hours, how sad and slow!"

His voice grew faint, and fixed was his eye
As if gazing on visions of ecstacy:
The hue of his lips and cheek decayed,
Around his mouth a sweet smile played —
They looked; — he was dead;
His spirit had fled,
Painless and swift as his own desire; —
The soul undressed
From her mortal vest,
Had stepped in her car of heavenly fire; —
And proved how bright
Were the realms of light,
Bursting at once upon the sight.

REST IN HEAVEN.

If ever life should seem
To thee a tedious way,
And gladness cease to beam
Upon the clouded day;
If, like the weary dove,
O'er shoreless ocean driven,
Raise thou thine eye above,—
There's rest for thee in heaven.

But O, if thornless flowers
Throughout thy pathway bloom,
And gaily fleet the hours,
Unstained by earthly gloom;
Still let not every thought
To this poor world be given;
Nor always be forgot
Thy better rest in heaven.

COMMUNION WITH GOD.

CHARLES WESLEY.

Thou hidden love of God, whose height,
Whose depth unfathom'd no man knows!
I see from far thy beauteous light,
Inly I sigh for thy repose;

My heart is pain'd, nor can it be
At rest, till it find rest in Thee.

Thy secret voice invites me still
  The sweetness of Thy yoke to prove;
And fain I would, but though my will
  Seems fixed, yet wide my passions rove;
Yet hindrances strew all the way,
I am at Thee, yet from Thee stray.

'Tis mercy all, that thou hast brought
  My mind to seek its peace in Thee,
Yet while I seek but find Thee not,
  No peace my wand'ring soul shall see:
O when shall all my wand'rings end,
And all my steps to Thee-ward tend!

What is there more that hinders me
  From ent'ring to thy promised rest,
Abiding there substantially,
  And being permanently blest?
O Love, my inmost soul expose,
  And every hindrance now disclose.

Is there a thing beneath the sun
  That strives, with Thee my heart to share?
Ah! tear it thence and reign alone
  The Lord of every motion there.

Then shall my heart from earth be free,
When it hath found repose in Thee.

Oh, hide this self from me, that I
No more, but Christ in me may live!
My vile affections, crucify,
Nor let one darling lust survive!
In all things nothing may I see,
Nothing desire or seek but Thee!

Oh Love, thy sovereign aid impart,
To save me from low-thoughted care;
Chase this self-will through all my heart,
Through all its latent mazes there:
Make me thy duteous child, that I
Ceaseless may "Abba, Father," cry.

Ah no; ne'er will I backward turn;
Thine wholly, thine alone I am:
Thrice happy he who views with scorn
Earth's toys, for thee, his constant flame.
Oh help that I may never move,
From the blest footsteps of thy love!

Each moment draw from earth away
My heart, that lowly waits thy call;
Speak to my inmost soul and say,
"I am thy Love, thy God, thy All."
To feel thy power, to hear thy voice
To taste thy love, be all my choice.

UNANSWERED PRAYER.

All night the lonely suppliant prayed,
All night his earnest crying made,
Till, standing by his side, at morn,
The tempter said, in bitter scorn,
"Oh peace: what profit do you gain
From empty words and babblings vain?"
'Come, Lord, O come!' you cry alway
You pour your heart out night and day;
Yet still no murmur of reply;
No voice that answers, "Here am I."

Then sank that stricken heart in dust,—
That word had withered all its trust;
No strength retained it now to pray,
While Faith and Hope had fled away;
And ill that mourner now had fared,
Thus by the tempter's art ensnared,
But that, at length, beside his bed,
His sorrowing angel stood and said,—
"Doth it repent thee of thy love,
That never now is heard above
Thy prayer, that now not any more
It knocks at heaven's gate as before?"

"I am cast out — I find no place,
No hearing at the throne of grace.

Come, Lord — O come! I cry alway,
I pour my heart out night and day,
Yet never until now have won
The answer — 'Here am I, my son.'"

"O, dull of heart! Enclosed doth lie,
In each 'Come Lord,' an 'Here am I.'
Thy love, thy longing are not thine —
Reflections of a love divine;
Thy very prayer to thee was given,
Itself a messenger from heaven.
Whom God rejects they are not so;
Strong bands are round them in their wo;
Their hearts are bound with bands of brass,
That sigh or crying cannot pass.
All treasures did the Lord impart
To Pharaoh, save a contrite heart:
All other gifts unto his foes
He freely gives, nor grudging knows;
But love's sweet smart and costly pain,
A treasure for his friends remain."

CHRIST, THE FOUNTAIN.

C. F. ORNE.

Lonely, oh lonely through the sands I wander,
The hot sirocco breath is on my brow;

Through every vein there runs a burning fever —
  Whither, oh whither shall I turn me now?

Where shall I seek amid the dreary desert,
  Where shall I seek a fountain pure and cool?
In vain my search, I only find the mirage,
  I only find some turbid, shallow pool.

Hither, poor wanderer; turn thy footsteps hither,
  Here springs a fountain, here cool waters flow;
Here quench thy thirst; who at this well-spring drinketh,
  No more, no more that burning thirst shall know.

Tell me, oh tell me, is this heavenly fountain
  By any holy, blessed name made known?"
"Christ is this fountain — Christ, the Lord's anointed,
  Sent from high Heaven, by the Holy One."

THE CRUCIFIXION.

MILMAN.

Bound upon the accursed tree,
Faint and bleeding,—who is He?

By the eyes so frail and dim,
Streaming blood and writhing limb,
By the flesh with scourges torn,
By the crown of twisted thorn,
By the side so deeply pierced,
By the baffled, burning thirst,
By the drooping, death-dewed brow,
Son of Man! 'tis thou! 'tis thou!

Bound upon the accursed tree,
Dread and awful,—who is He?
By the sun at noon-day pale,
Shivering rocks, and rending veil,
By earth that trembles at his doom,
By yonder saints who burst their tomb,
By Eden, promised, ere he died,
To the felon at his side,
Lord, our suppliant knees we bow;
Son of God! 'tis Thou! 'tis Thou!

Bound upon the accursed tree,
Sad and dying—who is He?
By the last and bitter cry,
The ghost gives up in agony;
By the lifeless body laid
In the chambers of the dead;
By the mourners come to weep
Where the bones of Jesus sleep;

Crucified! we know thee now—
Son of Man! 'tis Thou! 'tis Thou!

Bound upon the accursed tree,
Dread and awful,—who is He?
By the prayer for them that slew—
"Lord, they know not what they do!"
By the spoiled and empty grave,
By the souls he died to save,
By the conquest he hath won,
By the saints before his throne,
By the rainbow round his brow—
Son of God! 'tis Thou! 'tis Thou!

JACOB WRESTLING WITH THE ANGEL.

ATTRIBUTED TO CHARLES WESLEY.

Part First.

Come, O thou traveller unknown,
  Whom still I hold but cannot see!
My company before is gone,
  And I am left alone with thee;
With thee all night I mean to stay,
And wrestle till the break of day.

I need not tell thee who I am;
  My misery and sin declare:
Thyself hath called me by my name:
  Look on thy hands, and read it there.
But who, I ask thee, who art thou?
Tell me thy name, and tell me now.

In vain thou strugglest to get free,
  I never will unloose my hold;
Art thou the Man that died for me?
  The secret of thy love unfold;
Wrestling, I will not let thee go,
Till I thy name, thy nature know.

What though my shrinking flesh complain
  And murmur to contend so long?
I rise superior to my pain;
  When I am weak, then I am strong;
And when my all of strength shall fail,
I shall with the God-man prevail.

Part Second.

Yield to me now, for I am weak,
  But confident in self-despair;
Speak to my heart, in blessings speak;
  Be conquered by my instant prayer:
Speak, or thou never hence shalt move,
  And tell me if thy name be Love.

'Tis Love! 'tis love! Thou diedst for me,
I hear thy whisper in my heart:
The morning breaks, the shadows flee;
Pure, Universal Love thou art:
To me, to all, thy bowels move;
Thy nature and thy name is Love.

My prayer hath power with God; the grace
Unspeakable I now receive;
Through faith I see thee face to face;
I see thee face to face, and live;
In vain I have not wept and strove;
Thy nature and thy name is Love.

I know thee, Saviour, who thou art,
Jesus, the feeble sinner's friend;
Nor wilt thou with the night depart,
But stay and love me to the end:
Thy mercies never shall remove;
Thy nature and thy name is Love.

The Sun of righteousness on me
Hath risen, with healing on his wings;
Withered my nature's strength, from thee
My soul its life and succor brings;
My help is all laid up above:
Thy nature and thy name is Love.

Contented now, upon my thigh
I halt till life's short journey end;
All helplessness, all weakness, I
On thee alone for strength depend;
Nor have I power from thee to move:
Thy nature and thy name is Love,

Lame as I am, I take the prey;
Hell, earth, and sin, with ease o'ercome:
I leap for joy, pursue my way,
And, as a boundiag hart, fly home;
Through all eternity to prove,
Thy nature and thy name is Love.

HEAVENLY LOVE.

EDMUND SPENSER.

With all thy heart, with all thy soul and mind,
Thou must him love, and His behests embrace;
All other loves, with which the world doth blind
Weake fancies, and stirre up affections base,
Thou must renounce and utterly displace,
And give thyself unto Him full and free,
That full and freely gave himselfe to thee.

Then shalt thou feele thy spirit so possest
 And ravisht with devouring great desire
Of His deare selfe, that shall thy feeble brest
 Inflame with love, and set thee all on fire
 With burning zeale, through every part entire,
 That in no earthly thing thou shalt delight,
 But in His sweet and amiable sight.

Thenceforth, all world's desire will in thee dye,
 And all earth's glorie, on which men do gaze,
Seeme dirte and dross in thy pure-sighted eye,
 Compared to that celestial beauties blaze,
 Whose glorious beames all fleshly sense doth
  daze,
 With admiration of their passing light,
 Blinding the eyes, and lumining the spright.

Then shall thy ravisht soul inspired bee
 With heavenly thoughts, far above human skill,
And thy bright radiant eyes shall plainly see
 The idee of His pure glorie present still
 Before thy face, that all thy spirits shall fill
 With sweet entragement of celestial love,
 Kindled through sight of those faire things above.

THE CARE OF ANGELS OVER MEN.

SPENSER.

And is there care in Heaven? And is there love?
In heavenly nature to these creatures base,
That may compassion of their evils move?
There is: else much much more wretched were the case
Of men than beasts: But O th' exceeding grace
Of Highest God that loves his creatures so,
And all his workes with mercy doth embrace,
That blessed Angels he sends to and fro,
To serve to wicked man! to serve his wicked foe!

How oft do they their silver bowers leave
To come to succor us that succor want!
How oft do they with golden pinions cleave
The flitting skyes like flying pursuivant
Against fowle feendes to ayd us militant!
They for us fight, they watch and dewly ward,
And their bright squadrons round about us plant;
And all for love, and nothing for reward:
O, why should Hevenly God to men have such regard!

THE OMNISCIENT.

E'en now, while voiceless Midnight walks the land
And spreads the wings of Darkness with her wand,
What scenes are witnessed by thy watchful eye?
What millions waft to Thee the prayer and sigh!
Some gaily vanish to an unfeared grave,
Fleet as the sun-flash o'er a summer wave;
Some wear out life in smiles, and some in tears,
Some dare with hope, while others droop with
fears;
The vagrant's roaming in his tattered vest;
The babe is sleeping on its mother's breast;
The captive muttering o'er his rust-worn chain;
The widow weeping for her lord again;
While many a mourner shuts his languid eye,
To dream of heaven, and view it ere he die.
And yet no sigh can swell, no tear-drop fall,
But thou wilt see, and guide, and solace all.

COWPER'S GRAVE.

ELIZABETH B. BARRETT.

It is a place where poets crowned
May feel the heart's decaying —

It is a place where happy saints
  May weep amid their praying.
Yet let the grief and humbleness,
  As low as silence languish;
Earth surely now may give her calm
  To whom she gave her anguish.

O poets! from a maniac's tongue
  Was poured the deathless singing!
O Christians! at your cross of hope
  A hopeless hand was clinging!
O men! this man in brotherhood,
  Your weary paths beguiling,
Groaned inly, while he taught you peace,
  And died while ye were smiling.

And now, what time ye all may read
  Through dimming tears his story —
How discord on the music fell,
  And darkness on the glory —
And how, when, one by one, sweet sounds
  And wandering lights departed,
He wore no less a loving face,
  Because so broken-hearted —

He shall be strong to sanctify
  The poet's high vocation,
And bow the meekest Christian down

In meeker adoration;
Nor ever shall he be in praise
By wise or good forsaken;
Named softly as the household name
Of one whom God hath taken!

With sadness that is calm, not gloom,
I learn to think upon him;
With meekness that is gratefulness,
On God, whose heaven hath won him.
Who suffered once the madness-cloud
Towards his love to blind him;
But gently led the blind along,
Where breath and bird could find him;

And wrought within his shattered brain
Such quick poetic senses,
As hills have language for, and stars
Harmonious influences!
The pulse of dew upon the grass
His own did calmly number;
And silent shadow from the trees
Fell o'er him like a slumber.

The very world, by God's constraint,
From falsehood's chill removing,
Its women and its men became
Beside him true and loving!

And timid hares were drawn from woods
To share his home-caresses,
Uplooking in his human eyes,
With sylvan tendernesses.

But while in darkness he remained,
Unconscious of the guiding,
And things provided came, without
The sweet sense of providing,
He testified this solemn truth,
Though frenzy desolated —
Nor man nor nature satisfy
Whom only God created.

THE PATH TO HEAVEN NARROW AND THORNY.

COWPER.

The path of sorrow, and that path alone,
Leads to the land where sorrow is unknown;
No traveller e'er reached that blest abode,
Who found not thorns and briars in the road.
The world may dance along the flowery plain,
Cheered as they go by many a sprightly strain;
Where nature has her mossy velvet spread,

With unshod feet they yet securely tread,
Admonished, scorn the caution and the friend,
Bent all on pleasure, heedless of its end.
But He, who knew what human hearts would prove,
How slow to learn the dictates of his love!
That, hard by nature, and of stubborn will,
A life of ease would make them harder still,
In pity to the souls his grace designed
To rescue from the ruins of mankind,
Called for a cloud to darken all their years,
And said, "Go spend them in a vale of tears."
O balmy gales of soul-reviving air!
O salutary streams that murmur there!
These, flowing from the fount of grace above,
Those, breathed from lips of everlasting love.
The flinty soil indeed their feet annoys;
Chill blasts of trouble nip their springing joys:
An envious world will interpose its frown,
To mar delights superior to its own;
And many a pang, experienced still within,
Reminds them of their hated inmate, sin:
But ills of every shape and every name,
Transformed to blessings, miss their cruel aim;
And every moment's calm that soothes the breast,
Is given in earnest of eternal rest.

Ah, be not sad, although thy lot be cast
Far from the flock, and in a boundless waste!

No shepherd's tents within thy view appear,
But the chief Shepherd even there is near.
Thy tender sorrows and thy plaintive strain
Flow in a foreign land, but not in vain;
Thy tears all issue from a source divine,
And every drop bespeaks a Saviour thine—
So once in Gideon's fleece the dews were found,
And dropped on all the drooping herbs around.

THE THREE HOMES.

Where is thy home?" I asked a child
  Who, in the morning air,
Was twining flowers most sweet and wild
  In garlands for her hair;
"My home," the happy heart replied,
  And smiled in childish glee,
"Is on the sunny mountain side,
  Where soft winds wander free."
Oh! blessings fall on artless youth,
  And on its rosy hours,
When every word is joy and truth,
  And treasures live in flowers!

"Where is thy home?" I asked of one
  Who bent with flushing face,

To hear a warrior's tender tone
  In the wild wood's secret place;
She spoke not, but her varying cheek
  The tale might well impart;
The home of her young spirit meek
  Was in a kindred heart.
Ah! souls that well might soar above,
  To earth will fondly cling,
And build their hopes on human love,
  That light and fragile thing!

"Where is thy home, thou lonely man?"
  I asked a pilgrim gray:
He paused, and with a solemn mein
  Upturned his holy eyes,—
"The land I seek thou ne'er hast seen,
  My home is in the skies!"
Oh! blest—thrice blest! the heart must be
  To whom such thoughts are given,
That walks from earthly fetters free;
  Its only home is Heaven!

THE MOTHER AND DEAD CHILD.

She wrapped him in a little shroud,
  Her first born, and her last;
Her soul with heavy grief was bowed,
  Her tears were falling fast,
And ever and anon she prest
The icy burden to her breast.

She gently moved her trembling hand
  Up through his silken hair;
Her warm soft breath his sweet cheek fanned,
  But his was wanting there;
The hushed lips woke no joyous strain,
  Alas! they never ope'd again!

His full black eye was half unclosed,
  But faded was its light,
And on the drooping lids reposed
  Death's pale and mournful blight;
In winning tones she called his name,
But back a hollow echo came.

His infant toys along the floor
  Lay scattered far and wide,
Just as he left them there, before
  He laid him down and died;
The mother raised them, one by one,
  The treasures of her little son.

Within some safe and secret place,
  Those precious toys she hid,
Then calmly o'er his marble face
  She drew the coffin lid—
The pall's dark mantle o'er him spread,
But murmured not that he was dead.

Then slow his silent form she bore
  Beneath a willow tree,
Where once he loved to sit and pour
  A song of childish glee;
A bird sang on a bending limb,
Perchance it sung a dirge for him.

Below, deep in the flowery sod,
  A little grave was made;
Its very turf his feet had trod,
  For there he oft had played.
How felt that mother, as she gave
His play-ground for her darling's grave?

Her hand was firm, her cheek was pale,
  But blanched not with despair;
And sorrow only, winged the wail
  That rent the troubled air;
For it was but dust she gave the sod,
The gem she cherished was with God.

She scattered rose-buds on the spot,
   And lilies pure as snow,
Then turned and sought her childless cot,
   But spake not of her wo;
"In heaven," she cried, and sweetly smiled,
"The mother meets her seraph child."

PLAIN DEALING WITH A BACKSLIDING HEART.

REV. SAMUEL PEARSE.

Stupid soul, to folly cleaving,
   Why has God no more thy heart?
Why art thou thy mercies leaving?
   Why must thou with Jesus part?

Is there in this world existing
   Aught with Jesus to compare;
Yea, can heaven itself produce one
   Half so lovely, half so fair?

Ah! look back upon the season,
   When thy soul the Saviour chose
For thy portion, and thy spirit
   Did with his salvation close.

Ah! remember thine espousals;
  Didst thou not with Christ agree,
Leaving all thy former lovers,
  His, and his alone to be?

In his love thy powers exulting,
  What did all below appear?
Was there aught seemed worth possessing,
  Worthy of a hope or fear?

When thy heart, by grace instructed,
  Learnt the world to disesteem,
And to Christ for all resorted,
  Was there not enough in him?

Yes; thou know'st thy joyful spirit
  Knew no unfulfilled desire;
Longing still, and still receiving
  Fuel for the heavenly fire.

Why then, tell me, now so lifeless?
  Why this heavenly fountain leave?
Why to broken cisterns seeking;
  Cisterns, that no water give?

Doth not disappointment follow
  Every step that leads from God?
Have not piercing thorns and briars
  Shown their points through all the road?

Recollect, 'tis thus the Saviour
Says he will thy soul reclaim,
With weeping and with supplication,
Humbly offered through his name.

PERSEVERANCE.

A swallow in the spring
Came to our granary, and 'neath the eaves
Essayed to make a nest, and there did bring
Wet earth, and straw, and leaves.

Day after day she toiled
With patient heart; — but ere her work was crowned,
Some sad mishap the tiny fabric spoiled,
And dashed it to the ground.

She found the ruin wrought,
But not cast down, forth from the place she flew,
And with her mate, fresh earth and grasses brought
And built her nest anew.

But scarcely had she placed
The last soft feather on its ample floor,

When wicked hand, or chance, again laid waste
And wrought the ruin o'er.

But still her heart she kept,
And toiled again; and last night, hearing calls,
I looked — and lo! three little swallows slept
Within the earth-made walls.

What truth is here, O man!
Hath hope been smitten in its early dawn?
Have clouds o'ercast thy purpose, trust or plan?
Have FAITH, and struggle on!

THE EVENING STAR.

REV. W. G. DANA.

The evening cloud in Summer sky,
Reflecting the last light of day,
Appears all glorious to the eye,
But, soon dissolving, melts away.
When darkness has her mantle spread,
Those golden splendors all are fled.

But where that cloud in glory shone,
Whose hues so gorgeous did appear,
Gleams forth, where now that splendor's flown,

The *bright, unchanging* evening star.
That star serene forever glows,
Effulgent as when first it rose.

And so when Hope's fair visions fade,
Her radiant splendors seen no more,
When earthly scenes are wrapped in shade,
And life's illusions all are o'er,
A better hope then beams from far,
And shines, a *bright eternal star*.

THE SEA SHORE.

NEWTON.

In every object here I see
Something, O Lord, that leads to Thee;
Firm as the rocks thy promise stands,
Thy mercies countless as the sands,
Thy love a sea immensely wide,
Thy grace an overflowing tide.

In every object here I see
Something, my heart! that points at thee;
Hard as the rocks that bound the strand,
Unfruitful as the barren sand,
Deep and deceitful as the ocean,
And, like the tides, in constant motion.

TRUTH OF SCRIPTURE.

DRYDEN.

Whence, but from Heaven, could men unskilled in
arts,
In several ages born, in several parts,
Weave such agreeing truths? or how, or why,
Should all conspire to cheat us with a lie?
Unasked their pains, ungrateful their advice,
Starving their gain, aud martyrdom their price.

WORK AND CONTEMPLATION.

ELIZABETH B. BARRETT.

The woman singeth at her spinning wheel
A pleasant chant, ballad, or barcarolle;
She thinketh of her song, upon the whole,
Far more than of her flax; and yet the reel
Is full, and artfully her fingers feel
With quick adjustment, provident control,
The lines, too subtly twisted to unroll
Out to a perfect thread. I hence appeal
To the dear Christian church — that we may do
Our Father's business in these temples mirk,
Thus, stiff and steadfast; thus, intent and strong;

While, thus apart from toil, our souls pursue
Some high, calm, spheric tune, and prove our work
The better for the sweetness of our song.

INTERNAL EVIDENCE.

KITCHENER.

A man of subtle reasoning asked
A peasant if he knew
Where was the internal evidence
That proved the Bible true?

The terms of disputative art
Had never reached his ear,
He laid his hand upon his heart,
And only answered, "*Here.*"

EXTERNAL EVIDENCE.

Prophets of old, events foretold
Ages ere they transpired;
Each word fulfilled, as God had willed,
Proclaims they were inspired.

Wild tempests hushed; hell's counsels crushed;
The dead to life re-given;
All set their seal, that God's own will
Christ has revealed from heaven.

THE DEAD.

The dead alone are great!
While heavenly plants abide on earth,
The soil is one of dewless dearth;
But when they die, a mourning shower
Comes down and makes their memories, flower
With odors sweet, though late.

The dead alone are fair!
While they are with us, strange lines play
Before our eyes, and chase away
God's light; but let them pale and die,
And swell the stores of memory —
There is no envy there.

The dead alone are dear!
While they are here, long shadows fall
From our own forms, and darken all;
But when they leave us, all the shade

Is round our own sad footsteps made,
And they are bright and clear.

The dead alone are blest!
While they are here, clouds mar the day,
And bitter snow-falls nip their May;
But when the tempest-time is done,
The light and heat of Heaven's own sun
Broods on their land of rest.

DIVINE FOOT-PRINTS.

JEHOVAH-JIREH. — Gen. xxii: 14.

When thy faith is sorely tried,
Wondering how will God provide,
On his gracious promise lean,
In the Mount it shall be seen.

BETHEL. — Gen. xxviii: 19.

God is in the loneliest spot
Present, though thou know it not.
Morning vows and evening prayer,
Make a Bethel everywhere.

MAHANAIM. — Gen. xxxii: 2.

Go where duty guides thy feet;
There good angels thou shalt meet;
Hosts of God thou canst not see,
Watch thy steps and wait on thee.

PENI-EL. — Gen. xxxii: 20.

Dear and hallowed is the place
Where the Lord reveals his face;
Still he grants the blessing where
Israel prevails by prayer.

JEHOVAH-NISSI. — Exod. xvii: 15

What if foes the church assail,
Faith is mighty to prevail:
Pray, and Amalek shall yield;
God our banner in the field.

JEHOVAH-SHALOM. — Judges vi: 24; vii: 14.

When his saints are sore oppressed,
Gideon's sword shall give them rest;
God, who maketh wars to cease, —
God will give his people peace.

EBENEZER. — I. Sam. vii: 14.

Safely, through another stage
Of my earthly pilgrimage,

God has helped me: to his praise
I my Ebenezer raise.

JEHOVAH-SHAMMAH. — Ezek. xlviii: 35.

Zion, City of the Blest,
Happy seat of heavenly rest!
God's abode, where is no night, —
God its glory, Christ its light.

WHO GIVETH SONGS IN THE NIGHT.

[Job xxxv: 10.

When, courting slumber,
The hours I number,
And sad cares cumber
My wearied mind;
This thought shall cheer me,
That Thou art near me;
Thine ear to hear me
Is still inclined.

My soul Thou keepest
Who never sleepest:
'Mid gloom the deepest
There's light above.
Thine eyes behold me;

Thine arms enfold me;
Thy Word has told me
That God is Love.

A HYMN TO GOD THE FATHER.

DR. DONNE.

Wilt Thou forgive that sin, where I begun,
Which was my sin, though it were done,
Wilt Thou forgive that sin through which I run
before;
And do run still, though still I do deplore?
When Thou hast done, Thou hast not done,
For I have more.

Wilt Thou forgive that sin which I have won
Others to sin, and made my sin their doom?
Wilt Thou forgive that sin which I did shun
A year or two, but wallowed in a score?
When thou hast done, Thou hast not done,
For I have more.

I have a sin of fear, that when I've spun
My last thread, I shall perish on the shore.
But swear by Thyself that at my death Thy sun

Shall shine as he shines now, and heretofore.
And having done that, Thou hast done,
I fear no more.

NEARING HOME.

It is a pleasant thought,
And I say it o'er and o'er,
That I'm nearer home to-day
Than I ever was before;
Nearer my Father's house,
Where the many mansions be,
Nearer the great white throne,
Nearer the jasper sea,
Nearer the bound of life,
Where we lay our burden down,
Nearer leaving my cross,
Nearer wearing my crown.

MAN SHORT-SIGHTED.

BEATTIE.

One part, one little part, we dimly scan,
Through the dark medium of life's fev'rish dream;

Yet dare arraign the whole stupendous plan,
If but that little part incongruous seem;
Nor is that part perhaps what mortals deem:
Oft from apparent ills our blessings rise —
O then renounce that impious self-esteem,
That aims to trace the secrets of the skies;
For thou art but of dust — *be humble and be wise.*

THE CHANGED CROSS.

It was a time of sadness, and my heart,
Although it knew and felt the better part,
Felt wearied with the conflict and the strife,
And all the needful discipline of life.

And while I thought on these as given to me —
My trial tests of faith and love to be —
It seemed as if I never could be sure
That faithful to the end I should endure.

And thus, no longer trusting to his might,
Who says, "we walk by faith and not by sight,"
Doubting, and almost yielding to despair,
The thought arose — My cross I cannot bear.

Far heavier its weight must surely be
Than those of others which I daily see;
Oh! if I might another burden choose,
Methinks I should not fear my crown to lose.

A solemn silence reigned on all around —
E'en Nature's voices uttered not a sound;
The evening shadows seemed of peace to tell,
And sleep upon my weary spirit fell.

A moment s pause, and then a heavenly light
Beamed full upon my wondering, raptured sight;
Angels on silvery wings seemed every where,
And angels' music thrilled the balmy air.

Then One, more fair than all the rest, to see —
One to whom all the others bowed the knee —
Came gently to me as I trembling lay,
And "Follow me," He said, "I am the way."

Then, speaking thus, he led me far above;
And there, beneath a canopy of love,
Crosses of divers shapes and size were seen,
Larger and smaller than my own had been.

And one, that was most beauteous to behold —
A little one, with jewels set in gold;
Ah! this, methought, I can with comfort wear,
For it will be an easy one to bear.

And so the little cross I quickly took,
But all at once my frame, beneath it shook;
The sparkling jewels fair they were to *see*,
But far too heavy was their weight for me.

This may not be, I cried, and looked again,
To see if there was any here could ease my pain;
But one by one I passed them slowly by,
Till on a lovely one I cast my eye.

Fair flowers around its sculptured form entwined,
And grace and beauty seemed in it combined;
Wondering I gazed, and still I wondered more
To think so many should have passed it o'er.

But oh! that form, so beautiful to see,
Soon made its hidden sorrows known to me:
Thorns lay beneath those flowers and colors fair:
Sorrowing I said, "This cross I may not bear."

And so it was with each and all around —
Not one to suit my *need* could there be found;
Weeping, I laid each heavy burden down,
As my guide gently said, "No cross, no crown!"

At length, to Him I raised my saddened heart:
He knew its sorrows, bid its doubts depart.
"Be not afraid," he said, "but trust in me;
My perfect love shall now be shown to thee."

And then, with lightened eyes and willing feet,
Again I turned, my earthly cross to meet,
With forward footsteps, turning not aside,
For fear some hidden evil might betide.

And there, in the prepared, appointed way,
Listening to hear, and ready to obey —
A cross I quickly found of plainest form,
With only words of love inscribed thereon.

With thankfulness I raised it from the rest,
And joyfully acknowledged it the best —
The only one of all the many there
That I could feel was good for me to bear.

And while I thus my chosen one confessed,
I saw a heavenly brightness on it rest;
And as I bent, my burden to sustain,
I recognized my own old cross again!

But oh! how different did it seem to be,
Now I had learned its preciousness to see!
No longer could I unbelieving say,
Perhaps another is a better way.

Ah, no! henceforth my own desire shall be,
That he who knows me best should choose for me;
And so whate'er His love sees good to send,
I'll trust it's best, because He knows the end.

THE HEART'S CURE.

"Heart, heart, lie still!
Life is fleeting fast,
Strife will soon be past."
"I cannot lie still,
Beat strong I will."

"Heart, heart, lie still!
Joy's but joy, and pain's but pain;
Either little loss or gain."
"I cannot lie still,
Beat strong, I will."

"Heart, heart, lie still!
Heaven is over all,
Rules this earthly ball."
"I cannot lie still,
Beat strong I will."

"Heart, heart, lie still!
Heaven's sweet grace alone
Can keep in peace its own."
"Let that me fill,
And I am still."

FOUND IN A CASE CONTAINING A HUMAN SKELETON.

Behold this ruin! 'Twas a skull
Once of ethereal spirit full!
This narrow cell was life's retreat;
This space was thought's mysterious seat!
What beauteous pictures filled this spot,
What dreams of pleasure long forgot!
Nor love, nor joy, nor hope, nor fear,
Has left one trace or record here!

Beneath this mouldering canopy
Once shone the bright and busy eye —
But start not at the empty cell;
If on the Cross it loved to dwell;
If with no lawless fire it gleamed,
But with contrition's tear-drop beamed,
That eye shall be forever bright
When stars and suns have lost their light!

Here, in this silent cavern, hung
The ready, swift, and tuneful tongue!
If of redeeming love it spoke
Confessing Jesus' easy yoke,
If with persuasive mildness bold,
Condemning sin, of grace it told:
That tuneful tongue in realms above,
Shall sing Messiah's reign of love.

Say, did these fingers delve the mine,
Or with its envied rubies shine?
To hew the rock, or wear the gem,
Can nothing now avail to them;
But if the page of truth they sought,
Or comfort to the mourner brought,
These hands shall strike the lyre of praise,
And high the palm of triumph raise.

Avails it whether bare or shod
These feet the path of duty trod?
If from the bower of joy they fled,
To soothe affliction's humble bed;
If spurning all the world bestowed,
They sought the strait and narrow road,
These feet with angels' wings shall vie,
And tread the palace of the sky.

EPITAPH ON FOUR INFANTS.

ROBINSON.

Bold infidelity, turn pale, and die!
Beneath this stone four infants' ashes lie:
　　Say, are they lost or saved?
If death's by sin, they sinn'd because they're here;

If heaven's by works in heaven they can't ap-
pear:
Reason, ah! how depraved!
Revere the Bible's sacred page—the knot's untied:
They died,—for Adam sinned;—they live,—for
Jesus died.

HUGH PETER'S WISH FOR HIS DAUGH-TER.

I wish you neither poverty
Nor riches,
But godliness, so gainful
With content—
No painted pomp, nor glory that
Bewitches—
A blameless life is the best
Monument.
And such a soul as soars a-
Bove the sky,
Well pleased to live, but better
Pleased to die.

CHRIST THE SHEPHERD.*

[From the Spanish of Luis Ponce de Leon.]

BRYANT.

Region of life and light!

* * * * * * *

Nor frost, nor heat, may blight
Thy vernal beauty! Fertile shore,
Yielding thy blessed fruits for evermore!

There, without crook or sling,
Walks the good Shepherd! blossoms white and red
Round his meek temples cling;
And, to sweet pastures led,
His own loved flock beneath his eye are fed.

He guides, and near him they
Follow delighted: for he makes them go
Where dwells eternal May,
And heavenly roses blow,
Deathless, and gathered but again to grow.

*This piece is entitled The Life of the Blessed, and the second line is "Land of the good, whose earthly toils are o'er!" But as "nothing is beautiful which is not true," I cannot insert it as a picture of Heaven. Observe, however, how fair and just a description it is, of the incipient happiness of Christ's little flock here below.

He leads them to the height
Named of the infinite and long sought Good,
And fountains of delight;—
And where his feet have stood
Springs up, along the way, their tender food.

And when, in the mid skies,
The climbing sun has reached his highest bound,
Reposing as he lies,
With all the flock around,
He witches the still air with modulated sound.

From his sweet lute flow forth
Immortal harmonies, of power to still
All passions born of earth,
And draw the ardent will
Its destiny of goodness to fulfill.

Might but a little part,
A wandering breath of that high melody,
Descend into my heart,
And change it, till it be
Transformed and swallowed up, O love, in thee;

Ah, then my soul should know,
Beloved, where thou liest at noon of day,
And from this place of woe
Released, should take its way
To mingle with thy flock, and never stray.

MORNING HYMN.

ANNA JANE LINNARD.

Sleeper! awake and sing,
  The shades of night are gone;
Sleeper! awake and sing,
  The sun is hastening on,
He rises from his ocean bed,
Sleeper! arouse! lift up thy head.

Behold his glorious beams,
  Spread o'er the mountain top,
And now, like golden streams,
  Pour down its rocky slope,
The fields and trees are bathed in light,
The verdant earth with joy is bright.

The birds are on the wing,
  They warble forth their lays;
How sweet the notes they sing
  To their Creator's praise!
Sleeper, and canst thou silent be!
Has God, thy God, no claims on thee?

He watched thy slumbering hour,
  He guarded thee from ill;

His arm of love and power
  Is cast around thee still.
Oh, come, thy grateful offering bring;
Awake! awake! his goodness sing.

Each day its duty brings;
  Arise, and seek his face;
In him are all thy springs
  Of life, and strength and grace.
Awake! awake! His love adore,
His mercy seek, His aid implore.

ANOTHER.

DR. PARNELL.

See the star that leads the day,
Rising, shoots a golden ray,
To make the shades of darkness go
From heaven above, and earth below;
And warn us early with the sight,
To leave the beds of silent night.
From a heart sincere and sound,
From its very deepest ground;
Send devotion up on high,
Winged with heat to reach the sky;

See, the time for sleep has run,
Rise before or with the sun:
Lift thy hands and humbly pray
The Fountain of eternal day,
That, as the light, serenely fair,
Illustrates all the tracts of air;
The Sacred Spirit so may rest,
With quickening beams, upon thy breast;
And kindly clean it all within
From darker blemishes of sin;
And shine with grace, until we view
The realm it gilds with glory too.
See, the day that dawns in air,
Brings along its toil and care:
From the lap of night it springs,
With heaps of business on its wings.
Prepare to meet them in a mind
That bows, submissively resigned;
That would, to works appointed fall,
That knows that God has ordered all.
And whether, with a small repast,
We break the sober morning fast;
Or in our thoughts and houses lay
The future methods of the day;
Or early walk abroad to meet
Our business, with industrious feet, —
Whate'er we think, whate'er we do,
His glory still be kept in view.

O, Giver of eternal bliss,
Heavenly Father, grant me this:
Grant it all, as well as me,
All whose hearts are fixed on thee;
Who revere thy Son above,
Who thy Sacred Spirit love.

HYMN FOR NOON.

PARNELL.

The sun is swiftly mounted high,
It glitters in the southern sky;
Its beams with force and glory beat,
And fruitful earth is filled with heat.

Father, also with thy fire
Warm the cold, the dead desire,
And make the sacred love of thee,
Within my soul, a sun to me.

Let it shine so fairly bright,
That nothing else be took for light;
That worldly charms be seen to fade,
And in its lustre find a shade.

Let it strongly shine within,
To scatter all the clouds of sin,
That drive, when gusts of passion rise,
And intercept it from our eyes.

Let its glory more than vie
With the sun that lights the sky:
Let it swiftly mount in air,
Mount with that, and leave it there;
And soar with more aspiring flight
To realms of everlasting Light.

Thus, while here I'm forced to be,
I daily wish to live with thee;
And feel that union which thy love
Will, after death, complete above.

From my soul I send my prayer;
Great Creator, bow thine ear;
Thou, for whose propitious sway
The world was taught to see the day;
Who spoke the word, and earth begun,
And showed its beauties in the sun.

With pleasure I thy creatures view,
And would with good affection too;
Good affection sweetly free,
Loose from them, and wove to thee.

O, teach me due returns to give,
And to thy glory let me live;
And then my days shall shine the more,
Or pass more blessed than before.

HYMN FOR EVENING.

PARNELL.

The beam-repelling mists arise,
And evening spreads obscurer skies;
The twilight will the night forerun,
And night itself be soon begun.

Upon thy knees devoutly bow,
And pray the Lord of glory, now
To fill thy heart, or deadly sin
May cause a blinder night within.

And, whether pleasing vapors rise,
Which gently dim the closing eyes;
Which make the weary members blessed
With sweet refreshment in their rest;

Or whether spirits in the brain
Dispel their soft embrace again;

And on my watchful bed I stay,
Forsook by sleep, and waiting day; —

Be God forever in my view,
And never he forsake me too;
But still, as day concludes in night,
To break again with new-born light.

His wondrous bounty let me find,
With still a more enlightened mind,
Where grace and love in one agree —
Grace from God, and love from me, —

Grace, that will from heaven inspire —
Love, that seals it in desire:
Grace and love that mingle beams,
And fill me with increasing flames.

Thou, that hast thy palace far
Above the moon, and every star, —
Thou, that sittest on a throne,
To which the night was never known; —
Regard my voice, and make me blest,
By kindly granting its request.

If thoughts on thee my soul employ,
My darkness will afford me joy,
Till thou shalt call and I shall soar,
And part with darkness evermore.

THE PASSION FLOWER — A LEGEND OF PALESTINE.

J. H. BRIGHT.

Gone was the glory of Judea's crown,
And quenched that promised Star,
Before whose light the nations should fall down
And worship from afar.

And night came o'er Judea; deeper gloom
Shadowed that feeble throng,
That now to Carmel from the Saviour's tomb
Wound mournfully along.

Through the long moonless hours they lingered there,
Wet by the dews of even,
And on the viewless pinions of the air,
Their prayers went up to heaven.

And ever when the whispering breezes stirred
The pliant boughs of palm,
Or nestled in the trees the unquiet bird,
Breaking the midnight calm —

Their quick ears caught the melancholy sound,
And a dejected eye
Amid the deepened shadows wandered round,
As if their Lord drew nigh.

And then upon their aching sense would press
That loud unearthly cry,

Wrung from their Master, in his last distress
Of mortal agony.

Morn glowed upon the mountains; strange bright flowers
Like diamonds chased in gold,
That ne'er before had shone in fields or bowers
Their mystic leaves unfold.

And in each blossom, lo! the cross appears,
The thorny coronal;
The nails, the pillar, and the Roman spears,
A glory circling all.

Then, sacred flower! their grief was turned to praise,
And drooping sorrow fled,
Since He who bade thee bloom, they knew could raise
Their Saviour from the dead.

Three days within the grave's unbroken gloom
The hope of Israel slept,
Three mournful days around his guarded tomb
The holy watch was kept.

And from that hour, where'er thy buds expand,
Thou art of flowers the pride;
And nature's witness to all time dost stand,
Of Him, the Crucified.

RESURRECTION AND ASCENSION OF CHRIST.

DR. MARTIN MADAN.*

Hail the day that sees Him rise,
Ravished from our wishful eyes:
Christ, awhile to mortals given,
Re-ascends his native heaven.

There the mighty Conqueror waits,—
"Lift your heads, eternal gates;
Wide unfold the radiant scene,
Take the King of Glory in."

Circled round with angel-powers,
Their triumphant Lord and ours,
Conquerer o'er death, hell and sin,—
Take the King of Glory in:
Him, though highest heaven receives,
Still he loves the earth he leaves;
Though returned to his throne,
Still he calls mankind his own.

See, he lifts his hands above;
See, he shews the fruits of love;
Hark! his gracious lips bestow
Blessings on his church below:

*The cousin and friend of the poet Cowper.

Still for us he intercedes,
Prevalent, his death he pleads;
Next himself prepares our place,
Saviour of the human race.

Master, (may we ever say,)
Taken from our head to-day,
See thy faithful servants, see!
Ever gazing up to thee!
Grant, though parted from our sight,
High above yon azure height,
Grant our hearts may thither rise,
Seeking thee beyond the skies.

Ever upward may we move,
Wafted on the wings of love,
Looking when our Lord shall come,
Longing, gasping after home!
There may we with thee remain,
Partners of thine endless reign;
There, thy face unclouded see,
Find our heaven of heavens in thee!

WATERS TO SWIM IN.—Ezekiel xlvii: 5.

REV. RAY PALMER.

The ray of spiritual light upon
  The soul first beaming,

So passing sweet it is, he thinks,
He is but dreaming.
'Tis like a crystal fountain, whose young tide
In the parched meadows strives in vain to hide.

As onward in his course he goes,
His heavenly keeper
Leads him into a larger stream,
Broader and deeper —
And there he bids him his young limbs to try
As youthful birds their wings before they fly.

A little farther onward still,
This young believer
Finds that the stream has now become
A mighty river.
His sinewy arms the astonished swimmer plies,
And the *broad ocean* greets his wondering eyes.

FRAGMENT.

"O Lord, my God, do thou thy will—
I will lie still—
I will not stir, lest I forsake thine arm,
And break the charm
Which lulls me, clinging to my Fathers' breast,
In perfect rest!"

THE JOYS OF EARTH.

Few rightly estimate the worth
Of joys that spring and fade on earth;
They are not weeds we should despise,
They are not fruits of Paradise;
But wild flowers in the pilgrim's way,
That cheer, yet not protract his stay;
Which he may not too fondly clasp,
Lest they should perish in his grasp;
And yet may view, and wisely love,
As proofs and types of joys above.

"He went out into a mountain to pray, and continued all night in prayer to God." — Luke vi; 12.

Who art thou — on the midnight air
Pouring out thy lonely prayer?
Who art thou? — on the mountain still
Crying, "Father! do thy will"?
My God! my God! I see thee now,
The humid dews upon thy brow,
Thy longing eye, thy bended form,
Thyself all naked to the storm;
The forest pines about thee cast
Their greenness on the mountain blast —

The wandering stars, obscurely dim,
Hurrying draw their last rays in—
The captive clouds come black and torn—
The moon affrighted, veils her horn—
But thou, O Saviour! wrapt in love,
  Heedless of our nature's yearning,
Would draw my sense-chained soul above,
  Precept by thine act confirming.
Wake, my soul! up, up! and flinging
  All thy sluggish joys away,
Clasp the cross, and to it clinging,
  Of thy Saviour learn to pray!

THE CRUCIFIXION.

O that my eyes would melt into a flood,
  That I might plunge in tears for thee,
As thou didst swim in blood,
  To ransom me.
O that this flesh alembic would begin
  To drop—to drop a tear
For every sin!

See! how his pure, devoted arms are spread
To entertain death's welcome bands!

Behold his loving head! his bleeding hands!
His oft-repeated stripes! his wounded side!
Hark! how he groans! Remember how he cried.

The very heavens put weeds of mourning on;
  The solid rocks in sunder rent;
  And yet *this stone* will not relent!
    Hard-hearted man!
Only man denied — to mourn for him
    For whom alone He died!

HYMN BY A BENGOLI CONVERT.

KRISTNA PAL.

O thou, my soul, forget no more
The Friend who all thy misery bore.
Let every idol be forgot,
But O, my soul, forget Him not.

Renounce thy works and ways with grief,
And fly to this divine relief;
Nor Him forget, who left his throne,
And for thy life gave up his own.

Infinite truth and mercy shine
In Him, and he himself is thine:

And canst thou then, with sin beset,
Such charms, such matchless charms forget?

O! no! — till life itself depart,
His name shall cheer and warm my heart;
And lisping this, from earth I'll rise,
And join the chorus of the skies.

CONSECRATION.

Jesus, Saviour, Lord of Life,
We are thine, forever thine;
Toiling on with weary strife,
Help us with thy power divine!
When in battle fighting, bleeding,
Or in peace our flocks we're feeding,
By our side still abide;
Precious Saviour, ne'er forsake us,
Till to thy abode thou take us;
Then we'll cast our crowns before thee,
And in loftier strains adore thee!

Now we live for thee alone,
'Tis for thee these arms we bear;
Other leader we have none;
Sovereign Saviour, thine we are!

THE TRUE REST.

What dost thou, O wandering dove,
From thy home in the rock's riven breast?
'Tis fair, but the falcon is wheeling above;
Fly! fly to the sheltering nest.
To thy nest, wandering dove, to thy nest!

Frail bark, on that bright summer sea,
That the breezes now curl but in sport,
Spread swiftly thy sail, nor, though pleasant it be,
E'er linger till safe in the port.
To the port, little bark, to the port!

Tired roe, that the hunter dost flee,
While his arrow e'en now's on the wing,
In that dark green recess there's a fountain for thee;
Go, rest by that cool secret spring!
To the spring, panting roe, to the spring!

My spirit, still hovering, half blest,
'Mid shadows so fleeting and dim,
Ah! know'st thou thy Rock, and thy haven of rest,
And thy pure spring of Joy? Then to Him!
Then to Him, fluttering spirit, to Him!

THE CHILD'S GRAVE.

It is a place where tender thought
  Its voiceless vigil keepeth;
It is a place where kneeling love
  'Mid all its hope still weepeth;
The vanished light of all a life
  That tiny spot encloseth,
Where, followed by a thousand dreams,
  The little one reposeth.

It is a place where thankfulness
  Its tearful tribute giveth,
That one so pure hath left a world
  Where so much sorrow liveth;
Where trial to the heavy heart
  Its constant cross presenteth,
And every hour some trace retains
  For which the soul repenteth.

It is a place for hope to rise,
  When other brightness waneth;
And, from the darkness of the grave,
  To learn the gift it gaineth
From Him who wept, as on the earth
  Undying love still weepeth;
From Him who spake those blessed words —
  "She is not dead, but sleepeth."

A CHILD'S REQUEST.

A FACT.

" Mamma," a little maiden said,
  Almost with her expiring sigh,
" Put no sweet roses roses round my head,
  When in my coffin dress I lie."
"Why not, my dear ?" the mother cried,
  What flower so well a corpse adorns ? "
"Mamma," the innocent replied,
  " They crowned our Saviour's head with thorns. '

EPITAPH ON SUSANNA, WIFE OF DR. HALL, AND THE ELDEST AND FAVORITE DAUGHTER OF SHAKSPEARE.

Witty above her sexe, but that's not all,
Wise to salvation was good Mistris Hall.
Something of Shakspeare was in that, but this
Wholy of him with whom she's now in blisse.
Then, passenger, hast ne'er a teare
To weep for her that wept with all ?
That wept, yet set herself to cheere
Them up with comfort's cordiall.
Her love shall live, her mercy spread,
When thou hast ne'er a tear to shed.

THE BLIND BOY.

REV. DR. HAWKS.

It was a blessed summer day ;
  The flowers bloomed, the air was mild,
The little birds poured forth their lay,
  And everything in nature smiled.

In pleasant thought I wandered on,
  Beneath the deep wood's ample shade,
Till suddenly I came upon
  Two children who had hither strayed.

Just at an aged birch tree's foot,
  A little boy and girl reclined ;
His hand in hers she kindly put,
  And then I saw the boy was blind.

The children knew not I was near —
  A tree concealed me from their view —
But all they said I well could hear,
  And I could see all they might do.

"Dear Mary," said the poor blind boy,
  "That little bird sings very long ;
Say, do you see him in his joy,
  And is he pretty as his song ?"

"Yes, Edward, yes," replied the maid;
  "I see the bird on yonder tree."
The poor boy sighed, and gently said —
  "Sister, I wish that I could see."

"The flowers you say are very fair,
  And bright green leaves are on the trees;
And pretty birds are singing there:
  How beautiful for one that sees.

"Yet I the fragrant flowers can smell,
  And I can feel the green leaf's shade,
And I can hear the notes that swell
  From those dear birds that God hath made.

"So, sister, God to me is kind,
  Though sight, alas! he has not given.
But tell me, are there any blind
  Among the children up in heaven?"

"No, dearest Edward — there all see.
  But why ask me a thing so odd?"
"Oh, Mary, He's so kind to me,
  I thought I'd like to look at God."

Ere long, disease his hand had laid,
  On that dear boy so meek and mild;
His widowed mother wept, and prayed
  That God would spare her sightless child.

He felt her warm tears on his face,
  And said, "Oh, never weep for me:
I'm going to a bright, bright place,
  Where Mary says I God shall see!

"And you'll come there, dear Mary, too;
  But mother, when you get up there,
Tell Edward, mother, that 'tis you;
  You know I never saw you here."

He spake no more, but sweetly smiled,
  Until the final blow was given,
When God took up the poor blind child,
  And opened first his eyes in heaven.

A PERSIAN PRECEPT.

Forgive thy foes — nor that alone —
  Their evil deeds with good repay;
Fill those with joy who leave thee none,
  And kiss the hand upraised to slay.

So does the fragrant sandal bow
  In meek forgiveness to its doom,
And o'er the axe at every blow,
  Sheds in abundance rich perfume.

EARLY RISING.

MRS. SIGOURNEY.

Are my flowers awake,
That were sweetly sleeping?
Yes, they lift their heads,
Dewy tear-drops weeping.

Have the bees come forth?
At their work they're singing,
To the busy hive
Honeyed treasures bringing.

Is my birdling up?
Hark! his song he raises;
Let me join him too,
With my morning praises.

SONNET,

Written and addressed to Vasari, by Michael Angelo Buonarotti, A. D. 1557, when the author was eighty-three years of age.

Full nigh the voyage now is overpast,
And my frail bark through troubled seas and rude,

Draws near that common haven, where at last,
  Of every action, be it evil or good,
Must due account be rendered; well I know
  How vain will then appear that favored art,
  Sole idol long, and monarch of my heart.

For all is vain that man desires below :
  And now remorseful thoughts the past upbraid,
And fear of two-fold death my soul alarms,
  That which must come, and that beyond the
      grave;
Picture and sculpture lose their feebler charms,
  And to that Love Divine I turn for aid,
  Which from the cross extends his arms to save.

CLOSING STANZAS OF A HYMN.

SIR ROBERT GRANT.

The funeral pomp, superb and slow,
The gorgeous pageantry of woe,
The praise that fills th' historic roll,—
Can these assist the parted soul?
Or will remembered grandeur cheer
The shivering, lonely traveller?

And when that breathless, wasting clay,
Again shall feel the life-blood play,
When on the cell, where dark it lies,
A morn of piercing light shall rise,
O whither then shall guilt retire,
Or how avoid the eyes of fire?

O man, with heaven's own honors bright,
And fall'st thou thus, thou child of light?
And still shall heirs on heirs anew
The melancholy jest pursue?
And, born the offspring of the sky,
In folly live — in darkness die?

But I on thee depend, O Lord,
My hope, my help, and high reward;
Thy word illumes my feeble eyes;
Thy Spirit all my strength supplies;
In sickness thou my aid shalt be,
And death but gives me all to Thee!

THE PROSPECT OF DEATH.

REV. MR. EASTBURN.

When sailing on this troubled sea
Of pain and tears and agony,

Though wildly roar the waves around,
With restless and repeated sound,
'Tis sweet to think that on our eyes
A lovelier clime shall yet arise;
That we shall wake from sorrow's dream
Beside a pure and living stream.

Yet we must suffer here below
Unnumbered pangs of grief and woe;
Nor must the trembling heart repine,
But all unto its God resign;
In weakness and in pain made known,
His powerful mercy shall be shown,
Until the fight of faith is o'er,
And earth shall vex the soul no more!

SONNET.

BLANCO WHITE.

Mysterious Night! When our first Parent knew
  Thee from report divine, and heard thy name,
  Did he not tremble for this lovely frame,
This glorious canopy of light and blue?
Yet, 'neath a curtain of translucent dew,
  Bathed in the rays of the great setting flame,

Hesperus with the host of heaven came,
And lo! creation widened in man's view.
Who could have thought such darkness lay concealed
Within thy beams, O Sun? or who could find,
Whilst fly, and leaf, and insect stood revealed,
That to such countless orbs thou would'st us blind?
Why do we then shun death with anxious strife
If light can thus deceive, wherefore not life?

THE SOLITARY SUNBEAM.

The sunbeams infinitely small,
In numbers numberless,
Reveal, pervade, illumine all
Nature's void wilderness.

But, meeting worlds upon their way,
Wrapt in primeval night,
In language without sound, they say
To each — "God sends you light."

Anon, with beauty, life and love,
Those wandering planets glow,

And shine themselves, as stars above,
On gazers from below.

Oh! could the first archangel's eye
In everlasting space,
Through all the mazes of the sky,
A single sunbeam trace,

He might behold that lonely one
Its destiny fulfill,
As punctual as the parent sun
Performs its Maker's will.

SICKNESS LIKE NIGHT.

MRS. HEMANS.

Thou art like night, O sickness! deeply stilling
Within my heart the world's disturbing sound,
And the dim quiet of my chamber filling
With low, sweet voices, by life's tumult drowned.

Thou art like awful night! Thou gatherest round
The things that are unseen, though close they lie,
And with a truth, clear, startling and profouud,
Giv'st their dread presence to our mortal eye.

Thou art like starry, spiritual night!
  High and immortal thoughts attend thy way,
And revelations, which the common light
  Brings not, though wakening with its rosy ray
All outward life. Be welcome, then, thy rod,
Before whose touch my soul unfolds itself to God.

THE MARINER'S COMPASS.

See the magnetic needle lightly rest
  Upon its pivot — delicate yet strong;
  And (as the reeling vessel sweeps along,)
It trembles with the ocean's trembling breast.

A ripple moves it — easily depressed,
  But never conquered, though fierce whirlwinds
    roar;
  Again it points to a far distant shore,
Swayed by a spell unseen, yet still confessed.

And so the Christian on life's troubled sea,
  Forever shaken yet forever true,
Turns to the haven where he fain would be;
  His trials many, such his triumphs too;
Feels a mysterious power pervade his thrilling soul,
And with exulting faith obeys its strong control.

THE SUFFERER CHEERED.

"Say, shall I take the thorn away?" —
  So spake my gracious Lord —
"O'er which thy sighs are heaved by day,
  Thy nightly tears are poured?
Say, shall I give thee rest and ease,
  Make earth's fair prospects rise,
And bid thy bark o'er summer seas
  Float smoothly to the skies?

"Shall peace and plenty's cup swell high,
  Health leap through every vein,
And, all exempt thy moments fly
  From bitter inward pain?
Be naught to check the inspiring flow
  Of human friendship's tide;
And every want thy heart can know,
  Be quickly satisfied?

"Know thine ease-loving heart might miss
  The *comfort* with the *care!*
And that full tide of earthly bliss
  Leave little room for prayer! —
Few were thy visits to the throne,
  Unhastened there by pain;
Thou, o'er thy bosom-sins alone,
  Would'st small advantage gain!

"Nor deem the highest, holiest joy,
A stranger still to woe;
Blest servants in my high employ,
Most closely linked they go.
My love illumes with tenderest rays
The path of self denial,
And burning bright the glory's blaze
That crowns the fiery trial!

"In conscious weakness thou shalt hang
On my almighty arm!
Soon as the thorn inflicts its pang
I'll pour my love's rich balm,
Thou, plainest in thy deepest woe,
Shalt feel me at thy side;
And, for my praise, to all shalt show,
Thou art well satisfied."

LESSON OF THE SEA.

Go down unto the sea,
Where white-winged navies ride,
Whose mighty pulses heave so free
In strong mysterious tide—
Within whose coral cells,

Where sunless forests creep,
So many a wandering child of earth
Hath laid him down to sleep.

Go forth unto the sea,
And at the break of morn,
Teach its young waves the words of prayer,
Before the day is born;
And when the night grows dim,
Beguile the billows wild,
With the holy hush of thine evening hymn,
As the mother lulls her child.

Go — bow thee to the sea,
When the booming breakers roar,
And a meek-hearted listener be
To all their fearful lore;
And learn, where tempests lower,
Their lesson from the wave —
"One voice alone can curb our power,
One arm alone can save."

Go, homeward from the sea,
When its trial hour is past,
With deeper trust in Him who rules
The billow and the blast;
And when the charms of earth
Around thy bosom creep,
Forget not, in thy time of mirth,
The wisdom of the deep.

HYMN OF THE CITY.

W. C. BRYANT.

Not in the solitude
Alone, may man commune with Heaven, or see
Only in savage wood
And sunny vale the present Deity;
Or only hear his voice,
Where the winds whisper, and the waves rejoice.

Even here do I behold
Thy steps, Almighty! here, amidst the crowd
Through the great city rolled,
With everlasting murmur deep and loud —
Choking the ways that wind
'Mongst the proud piles, the work of human kind.

Thy golden sunshine comes
From the round heaven, and on their dwellings lies,
And lights their inner homes;
For them thou fill'st with air the unbounded skies,
And givest them the stores
Of ocean, and the harvest of its shores.

Thy spirit is around,
Quickening the restless mass that sweeps along;
And this eternal sound —
Voices and footfalls of the numberless throng —
Like the resounding sea,
Or like the rainy tempest, speaks of thee.

And when the hours of rest
Come, like a calm upon the mid-sea brine,
Hushing its billowy breast,
The quiet of the moment, too, is Thine;
It breathes of Him who keeps
The vast and helpless city while it sleeps.

THE CHRISTIAN IN THE CITY.

Love's a flower that will not die
For lack of leafy screen;
And Christian hope can cheer the eye
That ne'er saw vernal green.
Then be ye sure his love can bless
Even in this crowded loneliness;
Where ever moving myriads seem to say
Go—thou art naught to us, nor we to thee—away.

There are in this loud stunning tide
Of human care and crime,
With whom the melodies abide
Of the everlasting chime;
Who carry music in their heart,
Through dusky lane and wrangling mart,
Plying their daily task with busier feet,
Because their secret souls a holy strain repeat.

THE LORD IS IN HIS HOLY TEMPLE.

Be still, be still, for all around,
On either hand is "holy ground!"
The Lord of Hosts himself to-day
Is present while his people pray;
Bow down your hearts and kneel in fear,
In this his temple — God is here.

Bring no vain words, no wishes wild,
That best might suit an earth-born child;
Bid each unholy thought depart,
To heaven lift up a contrite heart.
Forget the world, in faith draw near,
And humbly worship — God is here.

Thou, tossed upon the waves of care,
Ready to sink with dire despair,
Gazing around with eager eye,
And yet no hope of remedy:
Ask thou relief with heart sincere,
And he will list — for God is here.

Thou who hast laid in early grave,
One, whom thou hadst not power to save,
And who art vainly yearning now,
For that soft smile and placid brow;
Perchance that much loved form is near,
For angels WAIT when God is here.

Thou who hast long a wanderer been,
Roaming through many a distant scene,
Far from thy home, thy household hearth,
From all kind looks, all social mirth;
Offer thy thanks with heart sincere,
Sing grateful praises — God is here.

Thou who hast dear ones far away,
On swelling seas, 'mid blinding spray,
Or in some distant lands alone,
Exposed to ills are journeying on:
Pray for their welfare, dry the tear,
And trust the God who listens here.

Thou, who art mourning o'er thy sin,
Deploring guilt that reigns within,
Seeking for higher joys than those
The wretched worldling only knows;
The God of *peace* is ever near
The contrite spirit bending here.

Be still, be still, for all around,
On either hand is "holy ground:"
Here, in his house, the Lord to-day
Will listen while his people pray:
Bow down your hearts and kneel in fear;
This is his temple — God is here.

THE THREE CALLS.

THIRD HOUR.

Oh! slumberer, rouse thee! Despise not the truth;
Give, give thy Creator the days of thy youth;
Why standest there idle! The day breaketh—see!
The Lord of the vineyard is waiting for thee!
"Sweetest Spirit, by thy power
Grant me yet another hour;
Earthly pleasures I would prove,
Earthly joy, and earthly love;
Scarcely yet has dawned the day,—
Sweetest Spirit, wait, I pray."

SIXTH AND NINTH HOURS.

Oh, loiterer, speed thee! The morn wears apace;
Then squander no longer thy remnant of graee,
But haste while there's time! with thy master agree;
The Lord of the vineyard stands waiting for thee!
"Gentle Spirit, prithee stay,
Brightly beams the early day,
Let me linger in these bowers;
God shall have my noontide hours;
Chide me not for my delay,
Gentle Spirit, wait, I pray!"

ELEVENTH HOUR.

Oh, sinner, arouse thee; thy morning has pass'd;

Already the shadows are lengthening fast;
Escape for thy life! from the dark mountains flee;
The Lord of the vineyard yet waiteth for thee!
"Spirit, cease thy mournful lay;
Leave me to myself, I pray!
Earth hath flung her spell around me,
Pleasure's silken chain hath bound me;
When the sun his path hath trod,
Spirit, then, I'll turn to God!"
Hark! borne on the wind is the bell's solemn toll:
'Tis mournfully pealing the knell of a soul —
Of a soul that despiseth the kind teachings of truth:
And gave to the world the blest hours of his youth,
The Spirit's sweet pleadings and strivings are o'er;
The Lord of the vineyard stands waiting no more!

BENEFITS OF PRAYER.

Lord! what a change within us, one short hour,
Spent in thy presence, will prevail to make!
What heavy burdens from our bosoms take;
What parched grounds refresh, as with a shower!
We kneel, and all around us seems to lower;
We rise, and all the distant and the near,
Stand forth in sunny outline, bold and clear;

We kneel, how weak! we rise, how full of power!
Why therefore should we do ourselves this wrong,
Or others — that we are not always strong;
That we are ever overborne with care;
That we should ever weak or heartless be,
Anxious or troubled, when *with us* is prayer,
And joy, and strength, and courage are *with Thee.*

AN OLD NEW YEAR'S POEM.

Though I be poore, yet will I make hard shift
But I will send my God a new yeares gift.
Nor myrrhe nor frankincense
Can I dispense,
Nor gold of Ophir
Is in my cofer;
With wealth I haue so small acquaintance as
I scarce know tinne from siluer, gold from brasse.

Orientall rubyes, emeralds greene,
Blew saphires, sparkling diamonds I haue seene,
Yet neuer yet did touch
Or gemme or ouche,
Nor pearle nor amber
Are in my chamber;

These things are in my mind, but neuer yet
Vouchsaf'd to lodge within my cabinet.

My euer liuing, euer longing King
Yet shall from me receiue a better thing;
For princes diademes,
Flaming with gemmes,
With richesse drest
Of east and west,
Match not this gift, wch if God shall owne,
I'll not change lots with him that weares a crowne.

An heart with penitence made new and cleane,
Fill'd with faith, hope, and loue, must be my strane.
My God, yt didst not slight,
The widowes mite,
Accept of this
Poore sacrifice,
Though I here give but what before was Thine
A treasure taken out of thine owne mine.

THE MOTHERLESS.

You'r weary, precious ones! your eyes
Are wandering far and wide;
Think ye of her, who knew so well

Your tender thoughts to guide;
Who could to wisdom's sacred lore
Your fixed attention claim?
Ah! never from your hearts erase
That blessed mother's name!

'Tis time to say your evening hymn,
My youngest infant dove!
Come, press thy velvet cheek to mine,
And learn the lay of love;
My sheltering arms can clasp you all,
My poor, deserted throng!
Cling, as you used to cling to her
Who sings the angels' song.

Begin, sweet birds, the accustomed strain,
Come, warble loud and clear; —
Alas! alas! you're weeping all,
You're sobbing in my ear!
Good night—go say the prayer she taught
Beside your little bed;
The lips that used to bless you then
Are silent with the dead!

A father's hand your course may guide
Among the thorns of life;
His care protect these shrinking plants
That dread the storms of strife:

But who upon your infant hearts
  Shall like that mother write?
Who touch the strings that rule the soul?
  Dear, smitten flock! — Good night!

TO SPRING.

Whence, oh sweet Spring, whence does thy balmy air
  Borrow such touch of sadness? And thy sky
So purely blue, so delicately fair,
  Why does it so bedim the earnest eye?

Alas, that gale o'er fairer flowers hath past
  Than those which now may meet our wishful gaze;
That sky with glory far too bright to last,
  Was gilded by the suns of other days.

Thou wak'st remembrances, and dim regrets,
  Summoning the lost—the absent—ours no more;
And every sun of thine before it sets
  Tells us of days and scenes for ever o'er.

'Tis then from memory's holy land thy breath
  Borrows such touch of sadness, and thy voice,

By her inspired, reminds our souls of death;
  Of blighted hopes and well-remembered joys.

And shall it not remind us too of hope?
  And bid us raise our sorrowing souls above?
Where the bright skies no tinge of sadness wear
  Through all the spring-time of eternal love.

DIRGE.

MRS. HEMANS.

Earth! guard what here we lay in holy trust;
  That which hath left our home a darkened place,
Wanting the form, the smile, now veiled in dust,
  The light departed with our loveliest face.
Yet from thy bonds undying hope springs free—
We have but *lent* our beautiful to thee.

But thou, oh Heaven! keep, keep what thou hast taken,
  And with our tears O keep our hearts on high!
The spirit meek, and yet by pain unshaken,
  The faith, the love, the lofty constancy,
Guide us where *these* are with our sister flown—
They were of Thee, and thou hast claimed thine own.

THE DEATH OF A CHILD IN APRIL.

(ADDRESSED TO ITS PARENTS.)

Say, is it spring in heaven, as now on earth,
  That tender buds should be demanded there?
That from your flow'rets of terrestrial birth,
  One, all acknowledged lovely, sweet and rare,
Should thus be called and safely borne away.
To ope its petals to celestial day?

You have one flow'ret less, and He one more:
  But yours must know the cold, and blight and storm;
His shall be nurtured where no tempests roar,
  No change nor death may touch the gentle form.
Then do not grieve when more to you are given,
To offer up one bud to bloom in heaven!

THE IDOL.

Whatever passes as a cloud, between
The mental eye of faith, and things unseen,
Causing that brighter world to disappear,
Or seem less lovely and its hope less dear,
This is our world — our idol, though it bear
Affection's impress or devotion's air.

HOME.

Thou, whose every hour
Is spent in home's green bower,
Where love, like golden fruit o'erhanging grows,
Where friends to thy soul sweet,
United, circling meet,
As lapping leaves that form the entire rose;
Thank thy God well — soon from this joy, thy day
Passes away.

Thou, at whose household fire,
Sits still thine aged sire,
An angel guest with lore as those of old;
Make thy young children's care,
That crown of hoary hair,
Which the calm heavens love as they behold:
Soon, soon the glory of that sunset ray
Passes away.

Thou, from whose household nooks
Peep forth gay, gleaming looks,
Those "fairy heads" shot up from opening flowers,
With wondrous perfume filled,
The fresh, the undistilled,
The overflowing bliss that childhood showers;
Praise Him who gave, and at whose word their stay
Passes away.

Thou, with another heart
United, though apart,

As two close stars that mingling shine but one —
Whose pleasant pathway lies
'Neath tender, watchful eyes,
Where love shines clearer than the morning sun;
Praise God for life, that in such soft array,
Passes away.

More, more — thou hast yet more!
These, thy heart's treasured store,
Transferred to heaven may win immortal birth
With radiant seraphs there —
May tune ambrosial air
To ever glorying hymns of praise, while earth,
Like lingering music from some harper grey,
Passes away.

HEAVEN.

When through the silent, midnight hours,
I watch with wakeful eyes,
And the frail clay's exhausted powers
Forbid my soul to rise;
Yet then, with child-like faith I cling
To my promise-keeping Lord;
I hide me 'neath his sheltering wing,
And stay me on His word.

There's calm in heaven, and perfect rest,
And undisturbed repose;
Sweet prospect to an aching heart,
Is such a peaceful close.
It's sweetness I delight to own,
But its purity is bliss,
I shall be like the Holy One,
And see him as he is.

RECONCILIATION.

Two celebrated ministers had quarrelled; they refused to speak to each other; when Dr. John Owen adopted the following plan to reconcile them, after several others had been tried in vain. He wrote and left at the house of each the following lines. An instant and perfect reconciliation was the happy result.

How rare that task a prosperous issue finds,
Which seeks to reconcile discordant minds!
How many scruples rise at passion's touch!
This yields too little, and that yields too much.
Each wishes each with other's eyes to see;
And many sinners can't make two agree.
What mediation, then, the Saviour showed,
Who singly reconciled us all to God!

TO MOURNERS.

HUIE.

O ye, who, with the silent tear,
And saddened step, assemble here,
To bear these cold, these loved remains,
Where dark and cheerless silence reigns;
Your sorrows hush, your griefs dispel,
The Saviour lives, — and all is well!

Those eyes, indeed, are rayless now;
And pale that cheek, and chill that brow;
Yet could that lifeless form declare
The joys its soul is called to share,
How would those lips rejoice to tell,
The Saviour lives — and all is well.

SEASONS OF PRAYER.

Come to the morning prayer:
  Come let us kneel and pray —
Prayer is the Christian pilgrim's staff,
  To walk with God all day.

At noon, beneath the Rock
  Of Ages, rest and pray;

Sweet is that shelter from the heat,
  When the sun smites by day.

At evening, shut thy door,
  Round the home altar pray;
And finding there the house of God—
  At Heaven's gate close the day.

When midnight veils our eyes,
  Oh! it is sweet to say,
I sleep, but *my heart waketh,* Lord,
  With thee to watch and pray.

ON GENESIS II: 21, 22.

CHARLES WESLEY.

Not from his head was woman took,
As made her husband to o'erlook;
Not from his feet, as one designed
The footstool of the stronger kind;
But fashioned for himself, a bride,
An equal, taken from his side:
Her place intended to maintain,
The mate and glory of the man;
To rest, as still beneath his arm,
Protected by her lord from harm,
And never from his heart removed,
And only less than God beloved.

TRUST IN GOD.

A dew-drop, falling on the wild sea wave,
Exclaimed in fear, "I perish in this grave!"
But, in a shell received, that drop of dew
Unto a pearl of marvelous beauty grew;
And, happy now, the grace did magnify,
Which thrust it forth, as it had feared, to die; —
Until again, "I perish quite," it said,
Torn by rude diver from its ocean bed;
O unbelieving! — so it came to gleam
Chief jewel in a monarch's diadem.

"AND THERE SHALL BE NO NIGHT THERE." — [Rev. xxii: 5.

No night in that bright land! Darkness shall fade
  Even with the beams of earth's faint sun away.
No twilight dim shall ever steal, to shade
  The glory of the everlasting day.

No night in that glad land! The gushing tear
  Shall swell no more beneath the grief-worn lid,
The cares, the fears, that bow the spirit here,
  Shall never breathe those courts of bliss amid.

No night in that free land! The fettered soul
Is bound no more as on the cruel earth;
It knows no master's wearisome control,
Serves only Him who gave it freedom's birth.

No night in Life's own land! The angel Death
Has gladly laid his mask of Terror down;
Mortality hath passed with mortal breath,
Unfading are the gems of Jesus's crown.

No night in that pure land! The monster Sin
No access to that holy realm shall gain,
No power to cloud those skies can ever win,
To whisper discord 'mid those songs again.

No night is there! but here our day is night;
Our brightest visions gleam amid the shade;
We know no rapture that is purely bright,
And scarce a hope that doubt cannot invade.

Father of lights! to Thee our longings turn;
Thou art the Sun of the eternal day;
By thee alone the stars immortal burn —
They but reflect Thy never-faltering ray.

Oh! in the depths of every human heart
Kindle the glow of Thine all-holy home,
And when from earth thou call us to depart,
Take us to that day — where no night shall come.

www.ingramcontent.com/pod-product-compliance
Lightning Source LLC
LaVergne TN
LVHW050530100826
845148LV00002B/510